PURSUIT
OF THE
CANADIAN
DREAM

A Guide for New Immigrants and Youth
To understand the Canadian Financial Landscape

AKINWALE THOMPSON, MSC, CFP®

Editing: J. Austin Lee Group, Bookbaby.

First printing edition: 2023

Print ISBN: 978-1-66788-806-4
ebook ISBN: 978-1-66788-807-1

Email: Akinwalethompson@gmail.com

TABLE OF CONTENTS

Acknowledgements	ix
Introduction	1
The Canadian Dream and the System	6
Risks and Rewards	9
Budget, Cashflow, and Net Worth	11

PART 1

17

Chapter 1: CREDIT	19
The Credit System	19
Credit Bureau	21
Developing a Credit History	24
Types of Credit	26
Overdraft Protection or ODP	26
Personal or Unsecured Line of Credit	27
Secured Line of Credit/Debt/Investment Loan	28
Student Line of Credit	29
Mortgages	30
Credit Cards	31
Different Ways to Manage Credit Cards	36
Predatory Lending	39
Installment Loans	39
Consumer Proposal and Bankruptcies	40
Consumer Proposal	40
Bankruptcy	41
Loyalty Programs	43

Chapter 2: CAR SALES AND LEASES — 45

Buying or Leasing Your First Car — 45

Chapter 3: BUYING YOUR FIRST HOME — 53

The Home Buyers' Plan — 56

Buying the House — 57

Three Ways to Pay off the Mortgage Quickly. — 59

Home Equity Line of Credit — 60

PART 2 — 61

Chapter 4: SAVING FOR UNIVERSITY OR COLLEGE — 63

RESP — 63

Lifelong Learning Plan — 65

Chapter 5: RETIREMENT — 67

RRSP or Group RRSP — 67

Lifelong Learning Plan — 69

Registered Retirement Income Fund (RRIF) — 69

Registered Disability Savings Plan (RDSP) — 70

Annuity — 71

Employer Pension Plans — 72

Locked-in Retirement Savings Plan (LRSP) and Locked-in Retirement Income Fund (LRIF) — 73

Employee Savings Plan and Stock Options — 74

Canada Pension Plan — 75

Old Age Security (OAS) and Guaranteed Income Supplement (GIS) — 77

Chapter 6: TAXES AND CHARITABLE GIVING — 79

Income Tax — 79

Goods and Service Tax (GST), Provincial Sales Tax (PST) and Harmonized Sales Tax (HST) — 80

Income Tax Filing — 82

Tax Avoidance   83

Tax Evasion   84

Charitable Giving   84

Chapter 7: INSURANCE   87

Life Insurance.   87

Term Life   88

Whole or Universal Life   89

Critical Illness (CI) Insurance: 91

Chapter 8: WILLS AND POWERS OF ATTORNEY   93

Wills   93

Power of Attorney/Living Will   94

Chapter 9: DEATH AND THE LOTTERY   97

Death   97

The Lottery   98

PART 3   101

Chapter 10: REAL ESTATE INVESTING   103

Principal Residence   103

Property Taxes   105

Buying Residential Rental Properties   106

Buying a Commercial Property   109

Buying New Build Condos   111

Buying a House on Acres of Land   112

Buying and Selling Land   113

Chapter 11: THE INVESTMENT LANDSCAPE   117

GICs (Guaranteed Investment Certificates)   117

Mutual Funds   119

How a Mutual Fund Works   119

Segregated Funds   121

Index or Indices   122

Exchange-Traded Funds (ETF)   123

Stocks (Shares)   124

Five Simple Ways to Analyze Stocks: 127

IPO (Initial Public Offerings)   128

Bonds   129

Investment Trusts   131

Brokerage   132

Discount Brokerage   132

Investment Advice and DIY Investing   133

Financial Plans   135

Insurance Advisor   137

Tax-Free Savings Account (TFSA)   138

Chapter 12: OTHER INVESTMENTS   **141**

Trading in Options   141

Short Selling   143

Cryptocurrencies   143

Forex Trading   145

Other Instruments   147

Chapter 13: BUSINESS OWNERSHIP   **149**

Sole Proprietor   149

Partnerships   150

Corporation or Limited Liability Company   151

Publicly Traded Companies   152

Starting Your Own Business   153

Your Business Plan   154

Buying a Business or Franchise   156

Chapter 14: RISK TOLERANCE   **159**

Chapter 15: FAITH   **169**

Chapter 16: CONCLUSION   **181**

Resources   **183**

Websites   **185**

    References   188

Glossary of Terms   **189**

    Credit   189

    Buying Your First Car   190

    Buying a Home   190

    Saving for University or College   191

    Retirement   191

    Taxes and Charitable Giving   192

    Insurance   193

    Wills and Powers of Attorney   194

    Death and the Lottery   194

    Real Estate Investing   194

    The Investment Landscape   194

    Other Investments   195

    Business Ownership   195

    Risk Tolerance   195

About the Author   **197**

ACKNOWLEDGEMENTS

To my wife, my love, my partner, and my greatest cheerleader, Lolade Leigh-Thompson, I appreciate all that you do for me; without you in my life, all these would not have been possible. Thank you for allowing me to share our stories of successes and failures with others and thank you for walking this journey with me. To my children, Temi and Tosin, I am so proud of you; you were my first readers, my unpaid editors, my finance students. Thank you for letting me test the ideas contained in this book on you, and I am glad you got it. I hope you will teach the lessons to others as well. To my father-in-law, Professor Abisogun Leigh, it was you who planted the idea of this book in me many years ago; you would constantly tell me to document my daily client experiences, "for a time will come when those experiences will help others and you might not remember them all." Thank you, Daddy, this is the fruit of that seed. To my cousin Folashade, a.k.a Aburo, the new immigrant, you came to Canada just after I finished the book; the questions you asked and the things you needed validated my ideas in the book. Thank you for being my test subject and for contributing your thoughts. To Rotimi Olumide, my brother and friend, you took the time to review, critic, and help stir the content in a better direction, thank you. To Gori Deen, my dear friend, the minute you heard about this work, you gave two concrete ideas that shaped the final outcome of the book; thank you. And finally, to Jabo, my brother from another mother, your friendship inspires me to do more; thank you for your listening ears. You and Mora's lives mirror ours on so many levels, and I know you can see yourself in the pages of the book; it's a pleasure to do life with both of you.

To my editor, J. Austin Lee, thank you for keeping track and thank you for being patient with me, and to my publishers thank you for getting this book out into the world.

INTRODUCTION

Most people hear of the "American Dream" and how everyone hopes to make it big some day in America. Canadians don't talk like that; few people talk about the "Canadian Dream." Perhaps, its because we don't have an all or nothing system. It doesn't mean that Canadians don't have big dreams and aspirations. After all, we are a prosperous nation, and we have a lot of successful corporations however a lot of people don't know how to achieve financial success in their personal lives.

This book is a guide for the new immigrants, youth, and anyone who seeks to better understand the Canadian financial landscape and navigate our economic systems. It's a resource to help you achieve *your* Canadian dream.

There are approximately 38.3 million people living in Canada, yet we are part of the Group of Eight (G8) nations. Over the past several years, immigration has been a top priority in our country. People come from all over the world to Canada, some speaking very little English or French, and many have settled here and made a decent life for themselves. While some came to escape terrible situations in their home countries, others came in search of a better quality of life—a better land, a land of opportunities, a land flowing with milk and honey. Some came for business, and others to work at the highest levels of their profession. While some have achieved these, others still struggle after years of living here to achieve it.

I am writing this book to my younger self, the twenty-nine-year-old who came from Nigeria in search of the Canadian dream. I was young and determined. I wanted it all. However, there was no one to guide and point me in the direction I wanted to go. As such, I began to experiment and study. I have engaged the credit system to the fullest and borrowed foolishly and wisely. I have been in substantial debt, and I have seen what freedom from debt feels like, and I still borrow. I have invested in all the different types of investments covered in this book, and I still invest. I have bought and sold several houses and still do so. I spent five years as a banker and sixteen years as a financial planner. This profession has allowed me to meet several people from various walks of life who are born Canadians or immigrants and multiple generations of them. I hear their incredible stories and see what they have done to achieve their dream, and it is with this perspective that I am writing this book.

In reflection of the country and my children being born and raised here, I noticed that my teenagers learned all they know about the financial system and how it works from me. Many of my clients bring their children to me to have a "Money Talk" when they start asking questions that the parent cannot answer. I looked at myself, an immigrant, and where I am, where I have been, and the number of mistakes I have made. When I taught classes to a primarily immigrant community, I took great pleasure when some had taken that knowledge and went on to do well in the system. When someone tells me they were able to buy or rent their first home, or they made money on an investment, made a contribution to their retirement plan, or started a business, it brings great joy to me.

I desire to ensure that all young adults and newcomers to Canada have the chance to understand how the Canadian financial system works. This book will help you navigate the system freely and avoid common pitfalls on your way to achieving *your Canadian dream*.

The first thing to know is that part of our charter of rights says that every individual is equal before and under the law and has the right to the equal protection and equal benefit of the law without discrimination and, in particular, without discrimination based on race, national origin, colour, religion, sex, age, mental or physical disability. So we accept people of all races and cultures. (www.justice.ca.gc)

Every immigrant who fulfills the "time spent in Canada requirement" can become a citizen, pursue their dream, and achieve whatever they desire. Once you become a citizen, you can vote or be voted for; you can become the prime minister, the governor-general, a businessperson, or city councillor. There are absolutely no restrictions on where you can live, work, or play. Therefore, it is important that you understand the system, especially the financial system, before you start using it.

This book addresses certain economic/financial terms and explains how it works in our society. It's not just a guide to the newcomer; anyone who seeks to learn about our financial and economic systems can benefit from this book.

While I have identified and discussed a few important topics, the book itself is in no way exhaustive, nor does it describe everything in detail. The intent is to help give you some understanding and the whys behind some of these things to engage them properly. If you require more knowledge of specific topics, I have included websites and other resources that can help you. Remember, you can always ask Google about the subject, and I am sure you will find a plethora of information.

How to Use This Book?

Though it's one book, I have divided it into three parts and used a lot of personal and client examples to buttress the points. The examples are all over the book in shaded boxes for you to follow easily. At the end of each chapter, I have also asked questions for you to use to check your understanding. The reason for this is that most people don't just pick up a finance book for no reason, and while money matters are important to all, some of the terms used in the world of finance can quickly be lost on even a keen learner. I have, therefore, tried to simplify the topic and content in as much everyday language as possible.

Part 1

Build your credit, buy your first car, and buy your first home.

The first three things a new immigrant or youth must grasp in their pursuit of the Canadian dream is the credit system (How to build it, how it affects them now and, in the future), how to purchase their first car if they need one, and how to buy their first home. The first three chapters delve right into these topics and will save you a lot of trial and error.

Part 2

Education, retirement, taxes and charitable giving, life insurance, wills and POA, death, and the lottery.

The next six chapters give you the bolts and nuts required in a proper financial plan, like how do you plan for children's education? What you need to know about the income tax system, Why do you need life insurance and what types do we have? Then we look at wills and powers of attorney, and the things to consider before death. The big lottery question is, *Can I just win the lottery and fulfill the dream in one swoop?*

Part 3

Real estate investing, investment landscape, and starting a business.

Perhaps, you are a little seasoned and would like to know about how you can own multiple real estate or other investment types like mutual funds, ETFs (Exchange Traded Funds) stocks, bonds, cryptocurrency, or forex trading, or how to start a business. What do you need to do? In Part 3, we review these topics and it serves as a guide for you to understand the rules of how it's done in Canada so that you can make informed decisions.

The chapters on risk, faith, and my conclusions are bonus chapters for you to get an insight into what I have observed and practised and let you know the source of my inspiration to see every new immigrant or youth fulfill their Canadian dream.

I hope you enjoy reading it like I enjoyed sharing it with you.

The Canadian Dream and the System

The Canadian dream is not a specific dream or limited to one thing or the other; it is whatever you dream of doing. You need to set a goal for yourself. What do you hope to accomplish in Canada? When you think about your life five, ten, or fifteen years into the future, what will be different? Some of us dream about career advancement, a big house, multiple real estate investments, cars, business owner-ship, stock portfolio, other investments assets, where and how to spend retirement, and more.

The Canadian Charter of Rights and Freedom (1982) shows the individual rights and freedoms we all have access to. Aside from that, I believe your dream is your dream and yours alone. There is nothing in life you dream of doing that you cannot achieve if you set your mind to do it, get the skills required, and patiently wait for it. Your Canadian dream can be anything you want it to be. However, hard work is not the only solution. You need to work smart and learn how to invest. You also need determination and patience. Our socio-capitalist nation teaches us that if you don't possess the skill you need, you should enrol in a college or school to learn it. There is governmental funding for immigrants to train or retrain in most post-secondary institutions; some are online, some are in-person—whatever your preference. You can also achieve it without school, but there's likely to be a lot of trial and error. Education is not limited to the four walls of a classroom or a certificate from studying and passing exams; it is what you have learnt, understood, and can apply.

So, try other forms of learning, like listening to podcasts or reading books on different subjects; you will be surprised at what you will gain, and somehow, as a life principle, opportunities always come your way when you are ready for it. Also, the harder you work, the luckier you get in life and the more successful you become. Someone once wrote that it takes 10,000 hours of practice on anything for you to become an expert at it. That would mean, it could take anywhere from four years of full-time to eight to ten years of part-time study to achieve proficiency in your field. People who go to a university can get a bachelor's degree in a subject. If they spend more time in the university, they get a master's and even a PhD.

I've met many highly educated immigrants who find it difficult to achieve their dreams. They talk about a roadblock called the "lack of Canadian experience." When I first heard the term "Canadian experience," my question was, *Is one plus one different in Canada than in Nigeria?* Just laugh it off and move on to the next person. Don't let anything or anyone steer you away from the dream you have imagined for yourself in this life or in this country. For those who are young or just returning to work after a prolonged absence to raise children, or any other reason, the recruiters have several responses for it: "You don't have good work experience, enough work experience, or recent work experience." Once you meet people like these, do them and yourself a great favour—move on. I have a friend who was off work raising children for eight years. When she came back and looked for work, and the work experience issue came up, she told the interviewer, "Apart from my qualifications from two universities in two different countries, I have worked with people on three different continents. I am a mother of two children. I have been married for ten years, and I manage my family responsibilities well." Most married people who have children, recognize the talents you need to stay married and have your children under your wings. Hey, she got the job! Your perspective of who you are is critical, and you should be able to verbalize it when asked.

Another important thing is to know the "Canadian System." This system is unique; it's different from that of other countries, especially of our cousins' south of the border.

Here is what I believe the Canadian System is designed to do. Please note that this is my perspective, and regardless of what it is, no system is strong enough to withstand the power of an individual's will. The Canadian system is designed for you to work hard. If you do, you will probably get promoted, earn a higher income, buy a home, get a mortgage, pay it off, have a vacation at least once or twice a year, possibly buy a cottage, pay it off, and send your kids to school. Then, when they leave the nest, you retire, sell your home, move to a retirement residence, and enjoy your life. You might even buy a vacation home in Florida and become a snowbird, who knows? Then pass on and leave your estate to the kids and grandkids.

If your desires in life are more than what I just stated or bigger than these, you must use the system and then work to "counter the system design" laid out for you to achieve a higher level of success. According to (www.reviewlution.ca) In 2021, Canada was home to 1.68 million millionaires and 64 billionaires. Canada had a total population of 37.59 million (www.worldpopulationreview.com). Compare this with the United States, according to Robert Exley Jr. (DEC 22 2021) US had 22 million millionaires and 724 billionaires. The US population was 332.9 million in the same period.

Risks and Rewards

I like to say that there are four major groups of people in the system:

1. Business owners, founders of corporations, and professionals in any field

2. Well-educated people who work hard

3. People who work hard but might not be well educated

4. People who don't work hard and are not well educated

This division is broad because we see various subsets that can exist in any system. However, my point is, the world we live in today is a world full of risks and rewards. Society rewards those who take risks more than any other group. Everyone has to invest in growing their assets, but we all fall into different groups and have different appetites for taking risks.

The first group includes everyone who has stepped out to start a business for themselves in any capacity: founders of corporations, professionals, trades, small businesses owners, and people who have followed a dream or thoughts of their heart to do something. They are the highest risk takers and often get rewarded the most. The first reward is the satisfaction of doing what they love and eventually succeeding in their chosen field. Taking risk by itself does not guarantee monetary success; other factors include being proficient in what you're doing, being patient, minding the money, et cetera. While people in entertainment and sports do not work for themselves in all cases, they fall into this first category. They are the brand, they produce, or what they do produces a very huge income for their employers, so they get rewarded with very high pay. This group has taken the first risk and can decide if they want to invest their high income in risky or non-risky assets. Still, they must invest in something other than the thing they do to diversify their risk and prepare for a future where they can no longer do that thing which produces the income.

The second group that gets rewarded is the "well-educated and works hard" group. Most people with higher education, professional certifications, and good work ethic get great jobs, get promoted, and earn a higher income, but they, too, need to invest in some level of risky assets to grow their investment and retirement assets.

The third group is the "work hard" group. These individuals may not have a lot of education. They also get promoted and earn higher wages, although usually with a cap on levels they can attain. They also need to invest in possibly risky assets to grow their investment and retirement assets.

The fourth group are those who did not attend school enough and who do not work hard. As a result, they do not make a high income, and it's difficult for them to invest in risky assets that will grow over a long time.

The people who are not in any of the groups above, fall on both the rich and poor sides. On the rich side are those who gain wealth by inheritance, lottery winnings and other unexpected windfalls and on the poor side are those who made a wrong investment, had health issues or things did not work out for one reason or the other. However, they also need to invest the inheritance funds in some level of risky assets to grow it and be able to give it to the next generation. On the poor side are those dependent on government welfare to survive. The Canadian social welfare is very strong and designed to keep children and seniors out of poverty. You should be able to get enough support to live if you are going through a rough patch or end up retired with a low income. Unfortunately, some young people and new immigrants get this support, which is supposed to be temporary. However, they stay on it until they become dependent on the system and cannot meaningfully get back into the workforce.

Therefore, regardless of whether you like it or not, we all fall into one of these groups, and we need to take steps to change the group we belong to by deciding to do today what will affect our tomorrow. We can pursue our dreams, we can go back to school, we can work hard and we can also buy life insurance today to change the financial situation of our next generation.

Budget, Cashflow, and Net Worth

We can't talk about money and not include the basics: Budget, Cashflow and Networth. It's required for your financial plan. What is a budget? It's a tabulation of your income and expenses over a specific period. This allows you to see all your expected expenses and the income you have available to pay for those expenses. Individuals use it, businesses use it, even governments use it. You can prepare a simple budget using a spreadsheet. You list your income for the month and all the expenses you have in that month—that's your monthly budget. If you then expand it month by month for a whole year, that's your family budget for the year. See a sample budget below, and you can find many templates online:

Budget 2022	January	February	March
Income			
Income 1	$4,000.00	$4,000.00	$4,000.00
Income 2	$3,700.00	$3,700.00	$3,700.00
Tax refund			$3,500.00
Total	**$7,700.00**	**$7,700.00**	**$11,200.00**
Expenses			
Tax on Income 1	$582.00	$582.00	$582.00
Tax on Income 2	$515.00	$515.00	$515.00
Mortgage or rent	$2,000.00	$2,000.00	$2,000.00
Car payment	$800.00	$800.00	$800.00
Cable	$65.00	$65.00	$65.00
Cell phone	$40.00	$40.00	$40.00
Car insurance	$380.00	$380.00	$380.00
Internet	$35.00	$35.00	$35.00
Gas	$300.00	$200.00	$250.00
Utilities	$170.00	$160.00	$140.00
Grooming	$60.00	$—	$20.00
Entertainment	$100.00	$200.00	$60.00
Life insurance	$220.00	$220.00	$220.00
Credit card payment	$400.00	$400.00	$400.00
Childcare	$140.00	$80.00	$200.00
Miscellaneous	$50.00	$50.00	$50.00
RESP (child education)	$200.00	$200.00	$200.00
RRSP (retirement plan)	$500.00	$500.00	$500.00
Total	**$6,557.00**	**$6,427.00**	**$6,457.00**
Cashflow			
	$1,143.00	**$1,273.00**	**$4,743.00**

You then continue this plan for twelve months and make plans to do something with the cashflow figure (which is the excess of income over expenses).

What I, however, want to show you is the cashflow budget (See below), this is what you will need monthly. It's a snapshot of your budget for just one month; you will enter figures in it and change it every time, based on actual income and expenses. So, while the budget is good for planning, the cashflow is used for managing your finances on a regular basis.

Once a year, preferably at the end of the year, you need to do another exercise, and that is, finding out your net worth. This is how much all your assets are worth, minus all your debts/liabilities at a particular time. If you do it at the same period every year, you will be able to track your path as you grow financially. Note that this is only supposed to be done once a year; there is an African gospel song that says, "Your blessings na double double o na double double." If you track your net worth, you will know if you are experiencing double, triple, or quadruple in your networth!

The following sheets, shows what a cashflow and net worth statement looks like.

Cashflow	First Two Weeks	Second Two Weeks	
Income			
After tax income 1	$3,418.00	$3,418.00	
After tax income 2	$3,185.00	$3,185.00	
Total	**$6,603.00**	**$6,603.00**	
Expenses			
Mortgage or rent	$2,500.00		
Food	$600.00	$1,000.00	
Car insurance		$380.00	
Car payment	$600.00	$600.00	
Cable	$—	$65.00	
Cell phone	$90.00	$—	
Internet	$—	$55.00	
Gas	$460.00	$300.00	
Life insurance	$220.00		
Credit card payment	$200.00	$200.00	
Utilities	$180.00	$160.00	
Grooming	$200.00	$260.00	
Entertainment	$220.00	$150.00	
Childcare	$260.00	$180.00	
Miscellaneous	$140.00	$200.00	
RESP (child education)	$200.00		
RRSP (retirement plan)	$250.00	$250.00	
Savings	$400.00	$400.00	
Total	**$6,620.00**	**$4,200.00**	
Cashflow	**$83.00**	**$2,403.00**	**$2,486.00**

Net Worth Statement			
Assets		**Liability/Debt**	
House	$700,000.00	Mortgage	$500,000.00
Car	$25,000.00	Car loan	$18,000.00
Jewelry	$6,000.00	Credit Card	$1,800.00
Electronics	$2,000.00	Line of credit	$2,500.00
Computers	$2,500.00		
Phones/tablets	$1,200.00		
Furniture	$7,000.00		
Retirement Plan (RRSP)	$17,000.00		
Savings	$25,000.00		
Stock portfolio	$28,000.00		
Total	**$813,700.00**		**$522,300.00**
Net worth		**$291,400.00**	

PART 1

Chapter 1:

CREDIT

The Credit System

The credit system for individuals is based on how people get and use credit. This information is published on two agencies' platforms and they are called the "Credit Bureau," and what you get from them is something called a "credit history."

There are two parties involved in a borrowing system: the "lender" who has the money and the "borrower" who needs the money. In a nutshell, the lender needs to confirm that the borrower will pay back the money borrowed at the agreed terms, and because they can't just take your word for it, they subscribe to the credit agencies' information. The credit agencies report a history of how the borrower has paid other lenders in the past. There are two credit bureaus or agencies in Canada (Equifax and TransUnion). If you want to do a financial transaction involving large sums of money or borrow in any capacity, the lender will consult these agencies to verify your credit history and to confirm your identity. In less developed countries, access to credit is based on your relationship with the bank manager and loan officers.

Some cultures don't believe in credit and don't use credit cards, mortgages, lines of credit, or overdraft protection. Some countries don't have the different kinds of investments like GICs (Guaranteed Investment Certificate), Mutual Funds, ETFs (Exchange Traded Funds), Index Funds, et cetera. These financial instruments might exist in other nations but are called by different names, like a car loan is called a car note or a GIC (Guaranteed investment certificate) is called a fixed deposit. When someone requests your credit history from the bureau, the term is called, "pulling or checking your credit." It means they are checking out your credit history with the two bureaus we have in Canada. Creditors will need your name, address, birth date, and social insurance number. These bureaus report your Canadian credit, and they are not linked up with any other credit bureau anywhere else in the world, even if they have the same name. Both mostly have information on all your credit applications, approvals, denials, and history of credit use. As long as you live here, most types of borrowing transactions would have required a credit pull. The Canadian banks have recently begun to request for people's credit history at the time they open a bank account.

Some people come from cultures or religious beliefs where it has been ingrained in them that credit is bad, so they stay away from credit use. They pay cash for transactions, and therefore, regardless of how long they have been here, they still have no history. Is it possible to do this permanently? Yes, you can; it is not much of a challenge when you own a business or substantial assets that you bring to Canada and can use cash to buy a home, but if you don't have that kind of money, you will definitely need credit at some point or the other. The average price of a three-bedroom townhouse in Toronto today is $1.24 million; in Vancouver, it is $1.29 million. So, if you have that kind of money, then you can stay off the grid. However, for all the regular folk, at some point, you'll need to buy real estate as part of your Canadian dream. Part of the approval process for a mortgage involves pulling your credit history. Also, you will need to do several things in this internet age that you cannot do without a credit card; booking airline tickets, making payments at certain places, and even getting a cell phone or utility requires a credit history request. The system here is a credit system, designed to allow you to do things conveniently, but without knowing the rules, you could quickly get into trouble. Most parents teach their children not to touch a live electric wire or run into the street, but so many of them don't teach their kids about finances. Kids don't learn about finances in school and the rules that govern our financial system is different from that in other countries.

Credit Bureau

The credit bureau is the central agency or a place where your credit is reported. They rate your credit usage on ratings from R1 to R9. An R1 rating means that you have made all payments on time and as agreed, R2 means you made a payment later than thirty days and less than sixty, and R3 upwards of sixty days to R9, which means you did poorly and did not pay on time or as agreed. The credit bureau uses these ratings and a complex algorithm that factors your amount of outstanding credit, the credit limits on your debts, the length of time for which you've had a credit bureau registration, and the number of credit facilities you have plus your income, to determine a credit score for you. This is the score that creditors look at in order to give you credit.

A score of 700+ is high and below 600 is poor or bad. Many creditors have a threshold score they are looking for to grant you credit. For example, a bank might require you to have a score of 700 to give you an unsecured loan at 4%; another bank will provide you with an unsecured loan for 8.5% because your score is 650. Likewise, a motor finance company might give someone credit to buy a car at an interest rate of 5% with a score of 720, and the same car company might sell the same car at a rate of 9% to someone with a score of 660. If you owe money to a cell phone company, a landlord, students loan, or any other loan, they can report the amount owed on your credit bureau if you refuse to pay. Therefore, when you have a dispute with a cell phone company or any creditor, it is wise to pay up first and then argue later than to allow them to tarnish your credit history. Once they book the report on your bureau, it is as though you have an issue with a company, and they announce to the world that you did not pay your loan or bill as agreed. Even if you resolve the issue, you cannot wipe out the memory from those who've heard it until time passes. In Canada, it is seven years. In the credit bureau, it takes seven years for any poor record to fall off after you've made the payment, and if you do not resolve it, it stays in your credit history permanently. When credit or loan companies see it, they might either not grant you credit or require you to first settle that matter before they consider you for the credit you want.

> *Tom was a high-income earner. After he finished university, a consulting company downtown hired him, and his income was over $100,000 per annum. Within a couple of years, his work required him to travel out of the country a lot, and because of his heavy schedule, he typically missed payments on his credit cards. Whenever he was in town, he paid them off. After five years of travelling, Tom was promoted to a managerial position, and he no longer needed to travel much. He decided to buy a house and settle down. It shocked him when his mortgage application was denied because of bad credit. It was not that Tom was a bad client or a poor client. He was not disciplined with his credit, and now that he needed to do something he could afford to do, his credit stood against him. Tom had to get a mortgage from a Grade-B lender at a higher rate.*

When someone wanted a new mortgage at a bank I worked at a few years ago, a similar situation occurred. The client's income was at a sufficient level; however, the credit report showed a cell phone bill that was outstanding or delinquent on their credit bureau. This bill was a result of a dispute with the phone company. So, we withheld funds from the borrower until the bill was paid. At times, in similar situations, the bank will mandate that part of the borrowed funds be used to pay the bill when advancing the loan.

Another factor that leads to lower credit scores is when you are credit shopping. Going from one institution to the next seeking all kinds of credit lowers your score drastically. Therefore, it is vital to keep your credit bureau clean, make all payments on time, and sign up for a service with the bureau that will alert you when anyone is checking your credit history. Be aware that no one has the right to check your credit history without your authorization.

Developing a Credit History

There are several ways you can develop a credit history; the fastest way is to get a cell phone. While it is not a credit card, cell phone companies pull a credit history before giving you a cell phone, and they can report late or delinquent payments to the bureau. If it applies to you, you may also take advantage of the new immigrant program at most banks to get a credit card within the first few months of arriving in Canada. When you are a young person, the banks will offer you a student Visa or MasterCard when you get into college. If you are none of the above, you can go to a department store like Canadian Tire or a furniture store like The Brick and buy an item and request that you want it on the store's credit card as long as you can pay a substantial part of the money required. Most stores will give you a credit card, which will help you create your credit history. It is called a credit history because it is the history of your credit usage. It is important how you use credit, not the amount of credit you have. For example, if you make your required monthly payment on or before the due date, you will develop a good credit history. Some people get a credit card, use it, and pay out the entire balance monthly. While that is good, when you have an established credit history and do not want to borrow money at high rates, it is not a good strategy when building a credit history. So, you must have a balance on the credit that you are paying and the lender is reporting, to show a history. Over time, as you develop a history, you will begin to get offers for different types of credit at reasonable rates. You should take them, use them, and thereby strengthen your history. It is almost as if these lenders are vouching that you are a good and upright member of society because you borrow money and pay it back on time. In addition, most employers these days require a credit to be pulled on their prospective new hire, especially if you are going to be working for a financial company. Most young people destroy their credit early because of a lack of understanding of how things work. Whatever you do, this is the number one financial planning tip for you as an individual. Make all credit payments as requested by the lender on time. When you start earning income, ensure that you prepare a rainy-day fund so that if you go through a rough patch, you don't fall behind on your bills or debt payment. The consequences of bad credit are not felt immediately. It is usually at a future date.

> *An excellent example of this is Judy, who was so scared of credit that she hardly ever used it when she got a credit card, and when she did, she went home and paid it off. Over time, Judy never got more credit as she did not need it. When it was time for her to buy a home, it wasn't easy to get her application approved even though she had money and could afford the house. Her credit bureau did not have a history of payments. What lenders are looking for is a CREDIT HISTORY.*

Types of Credit

Overdraft Protection or ODP

This is a credit facility attached to a bank account. It allows you to draw out more than your account's balance, up to the (credit) overdraft limit. The bank allows you to write a check for more money than you have in your bank account and put your account into a negative balance without a penalty. This covers unplanned debits or cheques that you did not remember to write in your check book. The bank does not want to return your cheque as Insufficient Funds (a "bounced" cheque, as we call it). If they do, they will charge you an NSF fee (non-sufficient fund) of $45. In most banks, you pay $4 per month ($48 per year) to have the ODP at an approximate interest rate of 21% for money borrowed, calculated daily and charged monthly. It is designed for extremely short-term use. It is not worth the cost of carrying it. The solution is to monitor your finances and ensure that you are not overdrawing your account. If you can save up an amount in your bank account and give yourself a buffer that you will not go below a particular amount, you will never need an ODP. It is an offence to write a check with no funds in your bank account, and you can be criminally charged for it.

Nakiso works in a department store and gets paid biweekly on Fridays. They automatically debit her car and mortgage payments from her bank account on the 1st of each month. Nakiso's income is just sufficient to make her payments. She wrote a check to an appliance repairman for $300 three months ago and assumed it had been cashed. The repairman had been busy with other work and did not get a chance to go to the bank. When he finally deposited the check, it debited Nakiso's account on the 1st of the month. So, Nakiso did not have enough to cover all her payments, and her car payment was returned for insufficient funds, and she was charged a fee by the bank and a penalty by the car finance company. If she had overdraft protection, all the transactions would have gone through, her account would have been in a negative balance till her next pay cycle, and she would only have to pay interest on the ODP for the time it was negative.

Personal or Unsecured Line of Credit

This is a revolving loan or credit facility offered to good clients at the bank. The interest rate is at prime rate + X, where prime is the rate the banks lend to their best customers and is universal among the banks and X is determined by the strength of your credit and relationship with the bank. You can draw down the credit line up to the maximum limit (amount granted), and you can pay back as much of it at any time without penalties and borrow from it again without a new application.

You are required to make a minimum payment each month based on your outstanding balance, usually 2–3%, by a certain date in the month. This is a better way to borrow. The downside is that if you carry a large balance, it will take you a long time to pay it off compared to a straight loan. An offshoot of the unsecured line of credit is a secured line of credit, usually with a home or investment.

When I was first developing my credit, I got offered a $10,000 line of credit (LOC) by the bank. I immediately accepted it. I used the facility to pay off all my outstanding credit card balances and began to make payments on the LOC monthly. Subsequently, different banks started to offer me similar credit facilities.

Secured Line of Credit/Debt/Investment Loan

This is like the unsecured LOC, except that the bank gives you the lowest interest rate possible because they have security that they can liquidate if you cannot pay.

I consider this a good debt for three reasons: you have the money, you are getting the best interest rate, and the interest on the debt becomes tax deductible if you invest the money. When a bank takes security, they usually give a credit facility of 80% to 90% of the security value unless it is a guaranteed investment, then they can give you credit of 100% of the security.

Some people use a LOC as a source of emergency funds; others use it to pay off outstanding credit card debt and then pay off the LOC, thereby taking advantage of the lower interest charges. In 2005, when the stock market was doing well, the bank I worked for offered its customers secured lines of credit against their investments. Most clients secured an amount equal to 80% of their balanced investment portfolio.

Student Line of Credit

This is a line of credit given to people going to college or university. It is usually at an interest rate of prime + 1% or prime + 2% and students apply for it jointly with their parents or guardians. I also consider this a good debt because you are investing in yourself. It is easy to get if you have been admitted to a recognized institution of higher learning and your joint signatory has proof of income. You do not make principal payments on the credit line while in school, only interest payments. After twelve to twenty-four months of graduating, you will start making principal and interest payments monthly. Hopefully, that is enough time for you to get a job and earn a good income. Therefore, it is important when using this option to pay for college that you study a course that will get you hired as soon as you graduate so that you can meet the payback schedule of the loan.

> *Shanaya was raised by a single mum and worked part time while going to university. She was able to use her income to pay most of her school expenses such that she finished university with no debt and got a better job. She worked for a couple of years, decided to do her master's in business, and got accepted into an MBA program at University of Toronto.. Although the cost was $60,000+ at the time, she was able to get a student line of credit and use it to pay for her course, and when she graduated, she got a higher income job and was able to start paying back the loan.*

Mortgages

A mortgage is a loan from a financial institution secured against real estate. Mortgages have terms and conditions. I consider mortgages a good debt as well, because like the secured debt, you are borrowing against real property that grows in value over time while living in and making payments for the house you will ordinarily have to wait for years to buy. The standard length of time for a mortgage (called Amortization) in Canada is twenty-five years; however, you can request for thirty years, fifteen years, and ten years. The period for which you get an interest rate called the "term," ranges from one to ten years. You can also get a variable rate or fixed-rate mortgage; as the name suggests, a variable rate has an interest rate that fluctuates with the prime lending rate while a fixed rate is a rate fixed for the term of the mortgage. Every time your term expires, you must renew your mortgage term. You should negotiate the rate for the term with your lender. And you should never accept a posted rate, or a rate sent to you in the mail at renewal, as these rates are suggestions, and you can get a sizeable discount by conversing with them. If you have enough equity in your home, you may be able to add a second and third mortgage to the current loan you have. These mortgages come in line as the second and third position to your original mortgage in the case of default. You can get a conventional mortgage when your down payment for your home is more than 20% of the value of the home or an insured mortgage if it is less. The CMHC and Genworth are the two major agencies that provide insurance for mortgages in Canada. The mortgage provider automatically applies for this insurance on your behalf if you meet the down payment criteria. They add the fees to your total mortgage loan, and you pay for it over time.

Mbappe had a home worth $800,000 and a mortgage of $200,000 with a bank. He wanted to start a business and needed seed capital. He found another lender willing to give him a second mortgage of $100,000 on the home. A year later, the business had grown but needed funds to meet a supply for one of their clients. So, he got another lender who gave him an additional $100,000 as a third mortgage. Because Mbappe had a lot of equity in his home, lenders were willing and gave him mortgages. Most times, you will find them lending up to 80% of the value of your home.

Credit Cards

There are five major types of credit cards:

1. Regular credit card

2. Secured credit card

3. Pre-paid credit card

4. Department or store credit card

5. Students credit card

1. **A regular credit card** is issued based on the general creditworthiness of the person requesting it. The bank or credit card company pulls a credit bureau report on you and determines if they will issue you a card and what the credit limit of that card should be. If you have good credit, you will qualify for this card, and they usually base the limit on the strength of your credit rating. Credit card interest rates range from 12% for some fee-based cards to 28%. A credit

card is not an effective way to borrow money based on its interest rate. However, it is a very convenient way to pay for goods and services. It offers a monthly statement that allows you to monitor your expenses, but it can become tough to pay it back if you carry a balance on it from month to month. A good recommendation is to make all payments on your credit card and pay your credit card balance every month or maintain a low balance if you are trying to develop a credit history.

Sade applied for a credit card with CIBC and was approved for $2,000. She has four bills every month, totalling $460, including her car insurance, cable TV, Netflix, and gym membership. She puts all the payments on her credit card, and every month on the 15th, she pays off her credit balance. If she is still in the credit-building phase of her life, she will maybe pay $300 into her credit card every month with a rolling $160 owed at the end of each month. She can then wait three to four months, pay it off, and continue the cycle. It will register well on her bureau, and her score will increase over time.

2. **A secured credit card** is a card where you use cash or an investment as security against your credit card. With this type of card, you are not really a risk to the credit card company as they have collateral that they can liquidate if you default. It is an excellent way to control spending and establish a credit history. The card shows on a credit bureau report as a credit card without indicating that it is a secured

card. So, if someone was establishing a new credit history or repairing bad credit, this card, when used well and paid as agreed, can help show a credit history which will eventually lead to other lenders offering you a regular credit card.

Ola is new in the country and needs a credit card for his daily activities, and he has $5,000 in his bank account. However, he could not get a credit card from his bank. So, he asked them to take $1,000 from his bank account and secure it against a credit card. The bank took the $1,000, invested it in a guaranteed investment certificate (GIC), and secured it against a Visa card which they issued to him immediately. As a result, Ola can now use his Visa card like any other Visa card and make all payments as agreed. Furthermore, if Ola uses this card well within a year or two, another institution will offer him a regular credit card, and he can cancel the secured Visa card.

3. **A pre-paid credit card** is not a credit card from a credit-bureau or history perspective. It is more a means of payment and convenience than anything else. For example, if you need to give money to a minor, you could load it onto a prepaid card, or if you are travelling to unsafe territories, you could take a pre-paid card or give it as a gift. Banks do not issue these cards. Instead, retailers like Walmart, Shoppers Drug Mart, et cetera, sell them.

> *Mr. Jung wants to buy a gift for his co-worker during a Christmas gift exchange. The budget is $50, but he does not know what kind of gift she will like, so he buys a $50 pre-paid MasterCard at Walmart. He gives her the card. She can use that card at any retailer the same way she will use any credit card.*

4. **A store credit card** is a credit card issued by department stores, furniture stores, hardware stores, and the likes. The card and its limit are based on the strength of your credit-worthiness, and the criteria to qualify for them are more relaxed than that of a regular credit card. This is because the stores are motivated to sell their products, and just like a car loan, they can repossess the furniture for non-payment. Moreover, because the criteria are lower, it can be an effective way to establish a new credit history or repair a bad one when used and paid as agreed. Stores, however, offer several deals where they ask you to make no payments for twelve months or twenty-four months. These deals are good for someone who intends to buy the product anyway and has the money to pay for it. Using time value of money calculations, if you pay anytime in the future for a product you use today, you can invest that money to get a return. It is, however, something to watch very carefully, as the fine print of these offers allows them to charge the total amount of interest you would have paid over the period if you did not fully pay for the product within the time stipulated, even if you only miss it by one day.

Roy and Angie got married, and were moving into their new apartment and neither has a credit history, but they have the cash to pay for their furniture. They saw an advertisement that there was a sale at Leon's Furniture and Home Depot. They went to both stores and found the furniture they liked, and both stores were offering a "don't pay for twenty-four months" deal. They asked for the deal and got it. This means the stores pulled their credit, found it was blank, and issued them a store credit facility. They went home with the furniture and now must pay off that loan before the end of twenty-four months. They have automatically established a credit profile.

5. **A student credit card** is given to college students over eighteen years old, and it is a card that allows them to start building a credit history. The problem is that no one takes the time to teach the new credit card holder about how credit works. It is like giving a loaded gun to a child and telling them to be responsible, without showing them what to do and what not to do. These include the following simple lessons:

A. Do not use the card beyond your credit limit.

B. Make at least the minimum payment before the due date.

C. Do not go on shopping sprees like you have free money.

D. All records of how payments were made on the card is available to any creditor.

E. How you make payments today will determine if you get other types of credit in the future.

Different Ways to Manage Credit Cards

A credit card balance transfer is an offer by your credit card company that they charge you a lower interest rate if you transfer the amount you owe at another credit facility. It is important to read the fine print on these offers to ensure you are not going from a bad situation to a worse one. First, you need to know how much interest rate they will be charging now and when the offer period expires. Then, you need to calculate the interest amounts and the transfer fee they charge for the offer, compared to if you were just making your payments. If there are no fees to do the transfer, it can be a good debt management tactic when you are trying to pay off all outstanding debt. Make your payments on time. I highly recommend that if your credit card company differs from your bank, then you make your payment at least three days before the due date. This allows enough time for it to be processed, so you do not have a record of late payment because of the bank's processing times. The bill payment from one bank to another may take two to three business days.

If you have a balance on your credit card, you must pay at least the minimum payment required each month to maintain a good credit rating/score, If you are late, it gives you a negative rating on your report even if you pay the full balance shortly thereafter.

However, paying the minimum payment on a credit card is one of the worst things that can happen to your finances because it keeps you owing for a very long time. Therefore, the government has mandated credit card companies to inform you about how long it would take to pay off your debt if you make minimum payments. You can find this information at the bottom of your monthly statement. For example, if you owe $2,000 on a credit card, it will take fifteen years to pay it off when you make minimum payments.

No matter how much you have in your bank account, the credit card is a separate relationship tracked continually for your creditworthiness. So, make your minimum payment or more before the due date, or if you can pay the entire balance by the due date every month, it will ensure that you do not carry a debt load. However, remember, using a credit card for purchases and then immediately paying it off is not the way to use it to develop a credit history.

Some credit cards charge an annual fee ranging from $50 to $200 in exchange for loyalty points. These cards are not for everyone, but the following illustrates how to use these cards wisely and effectively. If you want to get a card that gives points, get it during a credit card promotion. An example is the BMO rewards card; sometimes you get offered 10,000 points for signing up, and first year's fee is waived. CIBC Aventura and Royal Bank Avion are similar. These promotion points are enough to give you a short-haul flight to New York from Toronto. In addition, if you use your card for daily expenses and bills that you would normally pay with cash and then set up a pre-authorized payment to pay the entire balance within fifteen days of the payment, you will rack up points quickly without getting interest charges. One summer, we paid for our entire summer vacation to Disney World in Florida by using points. With these cards, the number of points can't fool you; the value of what the points can do is what matters. For example, 2,000 Air Miles can get two tickets to Boston from Toronto, while 50,000 points do the same with some Visa or Master cards that issue points. You need to check what each point pays for, how you get points, the value of the point in dollars, and most importantly, how much the annual fee is to make an informed decision.

Automate Credit Payment: A simple way to ensure you never miss any credit payment is to ask the credit company to automatically deduct the minimum payment from your bank account, then set up an overdraft protection loan on your bank account or make sure your account balance does not dip below a certain amount, that way you always have funds that will cover in case you forget.

Debt Payment Strategy: If you are already in debt and looking for how to pay it off, here are a few tips.

1. Get a part time job or an extra source of income.

2. Freeze credit use: Literarily freeze spending on your cards.

3. Make minimum payments on all credit and a larger payment on the credit that has the highest interest rate or tip 4 below.

4. Make minimum payments on all credit and a larger payment on the credit with the lowest balance.

5. Once one credit card/loan is paid off, add the larger amount you were paying to it, to the minimum payment

you were paying on the next credit/loan and start paying both to it, till you pay it off and repeat the process on the next card/loan.

6. Celebrate big every time one debt is paid to zero. It will fuel your determination for the next one.

7. Another option that rarely works is debt consolidation, where you get a loan to pay off all your debts and then you tackle that one debt. Most people end up right back were they started when they use this method. Although it works in theory, you have to know your personality and ability to keep a lead on spending.

Predatory Lending

Predatory loans are loans offered to desperate people, usually at extremely high-interest rates and conditions that will usually make it almost impossible to pay off and rob the borrower of any equity they might have. The criminal code in Ontario allows a maximum interest rate of 60%, while it is 30% in Quebec. The province regulates places like Payday Loans, where they charge the borrower about $15 to $25 on a $100 loan. These loans are only till the next paycheck in two weeks or a month; the math shows it's a 600% rate of interest if annualized.

Installment Loans

An installment loan is different and not regulated. Many mortgage brokers, lawyers, et cetera, offer these types with all kinds of fees and restrictive covenants, exorbitant penalties for missed payments, and tactics that could keep the borrower in debt for a long time. Be sure to know the conditions of the loan before you sign any agreement.

> *A client lost her job and could not find one before her Employment Insurance ran out. She maxed out all credit and eventually got a job paying less than half of what she previously made. She refinanced her home; it ended up with a predatory lender because her credit had gone bad. The mortgage interest rate was very high; she could not keep up with the payments and they eventually took over her home, and she had racked up more penalties that wiped out all the equity in her home.*

Consumer Proposal and Bankruptcies

Consumer Proposal

This is part of the Canadian Bankruptcy Act where a credit counselling agency takes over a debtor's credit situation, makes a total debt and income available to pay the debt calculation, and goes to each creditor and makes a proposal of how much the debtor can pay, which is usually cents on the dollar. The agency negotiates a fixed commitment to make those payments till the debt is paid off. Usually, they also negotiate a reduction in the debt outstanding in exchange for making regular monthly payments. It is a formal process where the agency takes on the role of the debtor and represents them with the credit companies.

> *Bruce Miller lost his job, and after the expiry of his employment insurance benefit, he still could not find a job. He had exhausted all his savings and had over $60,000 in debt. He could not keep up with the payments and still be able to pay rent and feed himself. Bruce reached out to a credit agency that determined his outstanding debt was $60,000 with two credit card companies, one furniture store and a bank. They also calculated that his obligated monthly payment was $1,600. They called each of the lenders and proposed different amounts and were able to reduce his total outstanding debt to $5,400; he had to pay $150 per month for thirty-six months to pay it off, after which they discharged him from all the debt. He will pay about $170 per month to the credit agency, and they will keep $20 for fees and expenses and pay the $150 to his creditors for the entire period.*

You should use these credit counselling agencies if you are overwhelmed by debt and do not know or cannot handle the constant calls from debt collectors. DO NOT USE the service to avoid paying debt that you might be able to pay off with some perseverance, hard work, and determination because the service they offer is still under the bankruptcy act and will show on your credit bureau for seven years. If you Google debt counselling, you will be sure to find an agency close to you.

Bankruptcy

This is a legal process and term where the debtor is declared unable to pay their outstanding credit listed, and all debts remain unpaid. They then discharge the bankrupt from the debt obligations.

The credit companies write off the debt, and most of them hardly ever lend to the bankrupt again in the future. There are many things a bankrupt person cannot do in society even after being discharged. Most professional associations will revoke licenses and not issue new ones to someone who has gone bankrupt while some employers will not hire them. If the bankruptcy was because of divorce, some employers might still consider offering them employment.

Jovan is self-employed and was making a lot of money. He bought many things on credit and was making payments until his business went down and he could no longer meet up with his obligations. Jovan owed $40,000 and had no money to pay it. He went to a credit agency and filed for bankruptcy. The agency listed all ten creditors and the amount he owed them and registered the bankruptcy.. Each creditor received the notice and, by law, discharged him from those obligations. He did not have to pay the debts anymore.

A bankruptcy declaration will remain on an individual's credit bureau for seven years, and most people will not lend to the debtor until it falls off their bureau record. Carefully consider these extreme measures and seek advice before entering them. Many credit counselling agencies can help for free. Certain Grade B and Grade C lenders still make loans to people who have used these methods to clear their debt by offering them credit with very high interest rates to reflect the risk of lending to someone who can suddenly turn around and declare bankruptcy.

A lot of people owe large amounts on credit cards because of the desire for instant gratification. It's easy to swipe the card, and it feels great to be able to get whatever we want when we want it. The high interest rate on the credit cards makes it very difficult to pay off the balance. Beware of storewide sales that encourage you to purchase what you cannot afford. The amount of savings on a 15% sale you get when buying something is less than the credit card interest paid when carrying the debt.

Loyalty Programs

Most retail stores or gas stations have a loyalty program where you get a card swiped for points when you purchase at the store. It is a way to reward you for being a loyal customer. You can redeem those points for in-store or online purchases when you accumulate enough points on the card. This is an effective way to save and earn because they also offer discounts or coupons to customers. The program does not cost you anything, and if you use the store regularly, you might as well earn something in return. You can sometimes double-dip depending on the credit card and who offers the reward.

Air Miles is a good loyalty program. For example, if you buy gas at a Shell station, you earn Air Miles every time you buy gas, and if your car uses premium gas, you earn two times the points. If you have an Air Miles card from any of the banks, you also earn points for using it anywhere, so if you use that card at Shell, you earn points twice, and from time to time, you get discount coupons on gas. You also earn Air Miles from many other retailers. By coordinating where you do your shopping, you can easily form steady habits to get enough Air Miles to get a flight ticket, hotel stays, or different goods, services, and gift cards from their website.

Test Your Knowledge of This Chapter:

1. What does your credit score do for you?

2. How do you develop a credit history?

3. When should someone consider a consumer proposal or bankruptcy?

4. Which debts are considered good debts?

5. What should you do with your bill, if you have a dispute with the service provider?

6. When should you pay your credit card bills?

Chapter 2:

CAR SALES AND LEASES

Buying or Leasing Your First Car

A car is one of the most expensive things most people will ever buy apart from a home. If you live in the city, you can probably get by using the subway and public transport, and it's cheaper than owning a car. However, if work, home, business, place of worship, or school requires a long commute, you might be better off owning a car. You must weigh the cost of your time, convenience, and other actual costs before buying a car. It is cheaper to use public transport in the city and join a shared car club like Zip cars and others to use a car and when it is necessary to have one, you can rent a car, such as when you must travel. Also, when filling out a credit application, at times, lenders ask you what kind of car you drive, the year and the model, then they ask you if you own your principal residence. It helps lenders to tell what kind of person you are.

If you decide to buy a car, there are several options. You can either buy a new car from a dealer, lease a new one from a dealer, buy a used car from a used car dealer, buy a used car from the owner, or take over a lease/purchase payment from someone who has one.

1. **Buy a new car:** This is the most expensive option; you must save a portion of the purchase price, and the dealer will get the car company's finance department to finance the remaining part of the purchase price. The interest rate charged for the purchase is usually very favourable because the manufacturer gets to sell their new car and loan you the money to do it. At different seasons, usually in the fall, when they try to clear out old inventory to introduce the following year's models, they offer incredibly aggressive interest rates like 0%. So, if your purchase time is flexible, you might want to wait till you see such a deal. A significant advantage of buying a new car is that you will have a manufacturer's warranty for a few years, and it will cover most repair issues that might come up.

> *Meera purchased a 2021 Honda Accord EX model in October 2020 for $40,000 taxes included, with 0% down and 0% financing for five years. It means that with a payment plan, the total purchase cost of the car over five years remains $40,000.*

2. **Leasing a car:** You do not own the vehicle in this option, but you lease it with monthly payments from the dealer/car company. The dealer is responsible for repairs; you pay for maintenance and get to use the car up to a maximum

fixed mileage per year. The higher the mileage amount per year, the higher your monthly payments. You also need to have a down payment to lease the car. The dealer will give you a buy-out option when your lease expires. An important thing to know is that you will be penalized if you go beyond the amount of mileage allotted to you. I had a friend whose lease was going to expire in six months, and they had already reached the maximum mileage limit, so they had to park the car and keep making lease payments, insurance, et cetera, until the expiration of the lease.

Greg leased a 2018 Range Rover Cruiser in October 2017. He paid a deposit of $7,000 and a monthly payment of $850 per month for two years with a maximum mileage of 24,000 km. At the end of two years, he returned the car. While he had the car, the dealer was responsible for the repairs and he the servicing.

3. **Buy a car from a used car dealer:** This option is risky and requires you to know about cars or get someone who knows about cars to assist you during the car hunting and purchase. The used car dealer deals with banks and lenders to finance your vehicle. They determine your interest rate based on your credit history and the amount of your down payment. Depending on the car's age and mileage, the dealer might sell you a limited warranty. You must expect these older cars to need repairs more frequently depending on age, make, and model. You must, therefore,

have access to a good and honest mechanic. If not, it can be the most expensive option. If you buy a used car that is three to four years old, most of the time, it is still as good as new, but if you buy a clunker or old broken car, you get what you pay for. The reasoning behind these is that cars lose their value (depreciate) from the moment you drive them off the dealer's lot. While some depreciate more than others, I have noticed that North American cars lose their value faster than European and Japanese cars. However, they cost less, and the cost of their car parts are cheaper, but they break down more often. In general, luxury cars retain their value better than cheaper, everyday cars. However, this is not a general rule there are certain exceptions, so do your research. Car websites like Autotrader.com will let you see the selling price of most cars based on the year and model.

Tony has $3,000 and needs a car. He cannot afford monthly payments of any kind on a car based on his income but will be able to pay for gas and repairs if they come later. He visits a used car dealership and finds a 20-years-old Lexus with a mileage of about 350,000 km listed for $3,500. He test drives the car; it seems good, and the body and inside are clean. He makes an offer to the dealer to buy it for $2,000. They negotiate back and forth and eventually settle at $2,500 + tax. The dealer does safety maintenance on the car, offers him a ninety-day warranty, and he picks it up two days later. If this car breaks down or has any major issues, Tony will be responsible for it. If you know little about cars, you can also pay your mechanic to look at the vehicle you want to buy or make him suggest a make and model that would be ideal before you begin your search.

4. **Buy a used car from the owner:** This option is very risky as you really do not know what you are getting; it is a hit or miss. However, this option is good when you do not really care about what you are getting; you just need a car to get around, and you are willing to take your chances. Some people maintain their cars very well and have a record of it. Others treat the car shabbily and are just looking for a buyer who will take it off their hands.

As a new immigrant I bought my first car from a friend who wanted to buy a new car because he just got a new job. I paid $600 for it, which was more than the car dealer would give him for a trade-in.

I drove it for two years without any major issues. Also another friend gifted me his old car, which the government valued at $100. I drove it for four years. When you buy a car from a private seller, you are required to pay tax based on the purchase price or value of the car when you are registering it in your name, also the car must pass a safety inspection.

5. **Lease or finance takeover:** Many people have taken out a lease on a car or financed its purchase and then lost their job, had to leave the country or find that they can't afford the payments. So, they use online sites like Leasebusters.com or Financebusters.com to find people who will take over their contracts.

I once had a colleague Jane who leased a car, and within four months of the lease, she got a new job where her apartment was across from the office building. She still had one year and six months to go on the lease where she had to pay $600 per month, while she hardly needed the car during the week and occasionally on weekends. She desperately needed someone to take over her lease payments.

If you choose to use this option, you must do your math right to ensure there is a value proposition for you and you are not just taking over a bad debt. A simple online calculator of lease payments will help you know if you are getting a better payment than going to the dealer to get a new car of the same kind yourself.

However, one thing to remember is that apart from the cost of car payments, you also must pay for car insurance and gas. As a new driver in Canada, insurance can be a bit expensive even if your car is cheap. Because you do not have a Canadian driving history, the insurance companies charge you a higher fee for the presumed risk they are taking.

When I owned the $600 car as a new driver, my insurance quote was $320 per month. I had to leave the car in the garage till, luckily, I got a job with a bank that owned an insurance company and they offered me an employee discount that made it affordable.

I had a young friend who bought a new car at age twenty-one. His car payment was $530, his insurance payment was $460, and he only had a part-time contract job. He did not know his insurance payments would be so high. I recommended he sell the car before he got into serious trouble.

In 2021 and 2022, because of supply chain issues, wait times for new cars was anywhere from twelve to eighteen months; the situation made prices of cars to rise. Car owners could now sell their used cars at a higher value than they paid for them due to demand, thereby flipping the concept that cars lose value the minute you drive out of the dealer's parking lot on its head. This is just an anomaly and is not expected to continue into the future.

Test Your Knowledge of This Chapter:

1.   When does the value of a car begin to go down?

2.   What should you consider before you lease a car?

3.   Why do lenders ask on a credit application about your car and if you own your principal residence?

4.   What happened to car prices after the pandemic and why?

Chapter 3:

BUYING YOUR FIRST HOME

Having saved up some cash or savings you brought with you to Canada, you must know that renting a home versus buying one is preferable when you are starting out or new to a city. You learn and understand where things are, which neighbourhoods are nicer, what the community is like, and the cost of housing. However, you should always have it in the back of your mind that this money is gone from your life forever once you pay rent. While you do not have to worry about repair, maintenance, and other expenses that a homeowner would worry about, you are sinking money into a hole. Therefore, I do not recommend renting long term, nor do I recommend renting expensive places, especially for a long period.

Once you start to earn a good enough income, the next step is to start looking into how to buy a home. The argument of "should I buy or should I rent," is thrown out the window because of the current rental prices. At the time of writing this, the average two-bedroom condo in Toronto rents for $2,700 per month plus utilities, If you move outside of Toronto, the same condo will sell for about $650,000. If you get a mortgage, your payments will be about the same price or slightly higher. While owning real estate is not a priority for everyone, you should consider that all rent payments are money lost forever, and mortgage payments will cease in time. In the process, your house value increases every year as your mortgage payment decreases every year.

> *Lucy and Dwayne Smith came to Canada from one of the Caribbean countries. They moved here in 1973, worked regular jobs, and began to save money to buy a house in the '70s. Their parents had taught them to not borrow money, so they used the bank to save money but not to borrow. When I met them in 2005, they were sixty-two and sixty-three. They had saved up $179,000 and were able to buy a condo around the Dufferin and Lawrence area. It took them thirty-two years to buy a two-bedroom condo with cash. In 2021, that Condo was worth $640,000.*
>
> *Mrs. Eskandar had also migrated to Canada from the Middle East in 1973, and when I met her, she was sixty-one years old. She also had a regular job and bought a house in downtown Toronto for $46,000 in 1975. She worked as a house cleaner on the side to earn extra money to pay her mortgage. She paid off her mortgage in 1995 (twenty years later). She had invested the money she used for her monthly mortgage payments and had accumulated about $90,000. When she became my client in 2005, her house was worth $850,000. In 2021, that same house was worth $3,150,000.*

> *While they had similar incomes and had been in Canada for about the same time, Mrs. Eskandar owned a home while the Smiths could only afford a two-bedroom condo. Mrs. Eskandar's house was in a neighbourhood that had become a sought-after location in Toronto, while the Smiths were just in an affordable area. Mrs. Eskandar had enjoyed the pride of ownership for well over thirty years before the Smiths did. The Smiths rented for thirty-two years, making their landlord richer and themselves poorer. If their rent was only $600 per month, they would have paid their landlord $360,000 over the years before they bought their home.*

The story of these two families is noteworthy. You must study and understand the system in any country you live in and use those systems to your benefit. The Smiths came from a country where you buy land, build a little portion of your house, and keep building from the extra income you have until you finish building. The process could take up to twenty-five years, but that's how you own a home; you don't borrow from the bank. Mrs. Eskandar, on the other hand, came from a country where people borrowed from the banks to build or own homes, so she wanted to own a home when she got to Canada. And as soon as Mrs. Eskander had a down payment saved up, she bought the home. Worth noting that Mrs. Eskander's house increased in value steadily from 1975 to 2005 and then to the whopping amount of $3.15 million in 2021.

Once you decide to buy a home, consider a few things. First, there is a better way to buy the first home that you may or may not have heard about. The Canadian government desires its citizens to own their homes, so a few systems exist that you should learn about to help make that dream a reality.

The Home Buyers' Plan

To help residents purchase their first home, the government of Canada allows would-be buyers to withdraw money from their RRSP (Registered Retirement Savings Plan, discussed a little later) with no penalty to purchase their first home. The maximum amount you can withdraw per person is $35,000 and, therefore, $70,000 per couple as of 2022. The goal, therefore, for anyone intending to buy a home is to first make contributions to an RRSP (Registered Retirement Savings Plan) every year till they reach or are close to this amount. When you contribute to an RRSP, you get a greater tax refund, which you can then re-contribute to the RRSP until you reach this savings goal. Please note that a withdrawal from RRSP under the Home Buyers' Plan is a loan from you to yourself and must be repaid into your RRSP, over a maximum period of fifteen years, beginning in the second year following the year of withdrawal. If you withdraw $35,000, you need to make an RRSP contribution of a minimum of $2,333.33 per year for fifteen years or risk paying tax on $2,333.33 every year if you fail to make an RRSP contribution. As discussed in the section on RRSP, it is wise to pay this amount back to your RRSP and more if you can. However, if you can't, the taxes on $2333.33 are not that high, compared to other benefits of owning a home.

> *I had a tenant who had saved up about $30,000 back in 2010 and was going to buy a house and knew nothing about the Home Buyers' Plan (HBP) or RRSP. I advised her to contribute $20,000 to her RRSP, get the tax slip, wait ninety days, and then buy the house and make the HBP withdrawal from the RRSP. She did this in January and bought the house in May. She used the tax slip on her income tax filing in March and got a total tax refund of $12,000, which added to her down payment for the house.*

Buying the House

You can hire a realtor (interview a few before settling on the one you gel with and understand their way of dealing with clients) or buy a brand-new house or condo from the builder directly. When you find a place that you like and the price is right for you, you make an offer. If it's a resale, the realtor will assist you and guide you on what to offer for the home you are buying; there might be a back-and-forth negotiation with the owner, and once you agree, you have a conditional offer. Most offers depend on you getting financing within one week, and the deal closes in thirty or sixty days, whatever time frame you the buyer and the seller negotiate.

Therefore, it is wise to engage a mortgage broker or your bankers to pre-qualify you for a mortgage before you start house shopping. That way, you know how much you can afford to buy based on your down payment and the likelihood of getting a mortgage. And, once you have a conditional offer, it's just a matter of two to three days for you to get a confirmation that a lender will provide you with the mortgage. Once you have a commitment from a lender to give you the mortgage and your home passes the home inspection, you can waive the financing and inspection clause and have a firm offer. You are also required to get home Insurance, after that all that is left to do is wait for the deal to close. To close in Canada, you need to send the firm offer to your lawyer, and your lawyer deals with the seller's lawyer and your financing institution. Your lawyer will close the deal and get you the keys to the house. Usually, the lenders will give them some conditions you need to fulfill, and they will calculate how much extra money you must bring to them, called closing costs. These costs could include land transfer tax, legal fees, title fees, et cetera, and can cost tens of thousands of dollars. It is a good idea to ask the lawyer for an estimate of the closing cost ahead of time so you can prepare for it. Closing costs can range from 1.5% to 4% of the house's value.

I know of a couple who bought a home for $565,000 and made a 5% down payment. They were happy they were finally going to move into their own house. A few days before closing, they got a message from the lawyer, telling them their closing cost was $31,000. They responded that they did not have the money. He told them they wouldn't be able to close and would lose the deposit they had paid to the builder two years earlier. Not wanting to lose the deposit and all the equity they had built up, they had to run around to raise the closing cost from friends and family.

If you are buying a new home from the builder, they typically have a fixed price for the house and an extra payment for all other things. In fact, after your deal is sealed and you go to choose the cabinets, paint colour, and other things the builder will put in your home, these upgrades can add a lot to the cost of the home. The builder will usually ask you to deposit a percentage of the purchase price of the home you have chosen to buy and more deposits over a specific period long before they even start to build.. Once you make a purchase and make the first deposit, send all the documents to your lawyer. Some new builds will take one to two years, and with some condos, it could be up to four years. The builder will ask you to come for a walk-through when the house is ready. This allows you to confirm that they have built as you wanted and painted the right colours, including flooring and things like that. The closing process is like a resale, as your lawyer will deal with theirs.

Remember that your first house does not have to be your dream home. It can be any type of house you can afford, which will get you out of the renting game.

Costs associated with home ownership includes but is not limited to the following: Mortgage payments, property taxes, home insurance, property maintenance, alarm or security monitoring, condo fees if you own one, utility bills and others depending on where you live, so be sure you have enough to make these payments before you buy the house.

Three Ways to Pay off the Mortgage Quickly.

Frequency of payments: Most mortgages are for twenty-five to thirty years, and you're required to make payments monthly. If you change the payment frequency to weekly or biweekly, you will shave off five to seven years of that time because interest on the mortgage is calculated monthly in arrears, so more frequent payments get to it before it is calculated. Also, by making biweekly payments for example, you get to make more payments than monthly in the two months of the year where you get an extra payment cycle in a month.

Lump sums: Practice making lump sum payments once or twice a year. You could schedule to make these payments when you get your tax refund or when you get some bonus at work.

Avoid refinance: While most people refinance within the first ten years of their mortgage, avoid it as much as possible even if the payment or interest rate is very attractive. if you have built up equity and you need the money, take out a home equity line of credit instead. The banks set up the amortization such that you make more interest than principal payments in the first ten years of your mortgage; so, if you refinance, you are resetting the clock again and paying more interest to the bank.

Home Equity Line of Credit

If you have a lot of equity in your home and you have an opportunity to pay off your mortgage and have a home equity line of credit instead **during a low interest rate period**, please do so. The home equity lines of credit are at the interest rates negotiated, and there are no weird calculations designed to keep you in the mortgage for any number of years, so you can pay off much of the principal with disposable income.

Test Your Knowledge of This Chapter:

1. When is renting good and when is it bad?

2. What happens to your mortgage in twenty to thirty years?

3. What is a Home Buyers' Plan?

4. What ways can you pay off your mortgage faster than the (amortization) agreed time?

PART 2

Chapter 4:

SAVING FOR UNIVERSITY OR COLLEGE

Post secondary education can be expensive in North America, so its wise to start saving for it, long before the time its needed. There are several systems in place to make it easier for you to afford post secondary school, two of which are:

1. Registered Education Savings Plan

2. Lifelong Learning Plan

RESP

An RESP (Registered Education Savings Plan) is a plan where you can save for university, college, or technical education for your children by investing with a promoter who offers these plans with allowable investments. There are several types of investments that you can have in your RESP, and different promoters offer different things;

be sure to choose the right investment that is in line with the risk you are able to take with your money. RESPs can be individual or family plans. An individual plan has one beneficiary while family plans have different members of the same family. The Government of Canada supports parents in their plan to save for children's educations, so the federal government pays a CESG (Canada Education Savings Grant) to the plan. This amount is equal to 20% on the first $2,500 invested, and additional grants are available for lower income families in the form of Canada Learning Bond.

The Canada Learning Bond is administered by the employment and social development Canada (ESDC). They provide an additional $2,000 to encourage low-income families to start saving early for their child's higher education, and the money is deposited directly to the RESP plan. Children who were born in 2004 or later get an initial payment of $500 and then $100 for each year till they turn fifteen. You are not required to make an RESP contribution to get the CLB (Canada Learning Bond) so technically speaking, the initial $500 and the subsequent payments up to $2,000 is free money. As a new immigrant, you don't know what your income will be later on, so it's advisable that you apply for this bond the minute your child is eligible (lives here and has a social insurance number). The maximum amount of CESG you can get over the life of the RESP plan is $7,200 and the maximum amount that can be contributed to an RESP is $50,000. You only receive grants up to the year that the beneficiary turns seventeen, but contributions can be made in a family plan for any beneficiary under the age of thirty-one.

An advantage of the family plan is that if any of the beneficiaries decides not to go to school for whatever reasons, any of the siblings in the plan can use the funds in the plan for higher education.

The Quebec and BC governments also pay an additional grant to the RESPS in their province. To qualify for the grant, all your child needs is to be a resident of Canada and have a social insurance number. The higher education school can be in Canada or abroad, as long as they meet some specific criteria as to the length of the program and the number of hours of lectures per week. Please note that the invested contributions and growth are withdrawn and given to the child while the grant portion is paid directly to the child when it's time to go to college or university.

All the banks, insurance companies, and mutual fund companies have RESPs sold by their advisors. A few institutions sell RESP plans alone, so make sure you review your options, and please note that regardless of where you started your RESP, you can transfer it to another institution at any time. When you are opening the account, please confirm that there are no fees attached to the account that can prevent a meaningful transfer if you change your mind about the institution in the future.

Lifelong Learning Plan

This plan allows you to withdraw money from your own or spouse's retirement savings plan (RRSP) (discussed in Chapter 5), to finance full-time post-secondary education. The funds must have been in your RRSP for at least ninety days before you use it, and the maximum per calendar year is $10,000, and the limit that can be withdrawn is $20,000. It does not mandate that the money be used for tuition expenses only; you can use it for other costs. If you meet the criteria, you can withdraw over four years, and you must repay it over ten years by contributing one-tenth of the amount to your retirement savings plan (RRSP)

When Dikembe did his Master's in Finance, his employment income was too high for him to qualify for any government loan. However, he had money in his RRSP, so he requested a withdrawal of $20,000 from his RRSP over two years and was able to use it as part of his tuition payment. Now he pays it back through his RRSP contribution yearly. If he does not make an RRSP contribution of at least $2,000 per year, he will need to add $2,000 to his taxable income for that year.

Test Your Knowledge of This Chapter:

1. What percentage does the government contribute to an RESP plan for every dollar you invest?

2. If someone is a low-income earner, what amount does the government contribute to their RESP even if they don't invest?

3. How much can you withdraw from your RRSP to fund your university or college education?

4. What is lifelong learning withdrawal?

Chapter 5:

RETIREMENT

Once you get a regular job, it is worthwhile to start thinking of the day when you will retire. When you plan for retirement early, you require much less in regular savings to reach the financial goal than when you start late. Most immigrants come here in their thirties and forties, so the earlier you start, the better. If you are in your twenties, you are in a sweet spot. Most banks and financial advisors can show you simple calculations that show how much you must invest each month to reach a future goal (there are also a few calculators on Google). By investing a fixed amount every week, every two weeks, or every month for a long period of time, you can achieve whatever retirement goals you set for yourself. You can fund your retirement by investing in RRSPs, TFSA, permanent life insurance policies, investment properties, non-registered investments and businesses.

RRSP or Group RRSP

The government allows you to contribute 18% of your last year's income to a Registered Retirement Savings Plan (RRSP) up to a maximum of $29,210 as of 2022. When you do, the financial institution where you contributed will issue you a tax receipt (contribution slip). Then, when you file this receipt with your income tax, you get a bigger tax refund as your income is reduced by the amount of the receipt, and any taxes you had paid on the higher income will be refunded to you. In addition, the money within an RRSP plan also grows on a tax-deferred basis, meaning you do not pay taxes on the growth of your investments within the RRSP account.

Some corporations offer group RRSPs to their employees. You can tell your employer to make automatic contributions to your RRSP from your pay before calculating the income tax. It gives you a better cash flow and the benefit of automatic savings, not a refund. You can invest in an RRSP until age seventy-one, when the RRSP must be collapsed or converted. RRSPs are not protected from creditors and are part of family assets in case of divorce settlements. If you withdraw money from an RRSP, the institution will withhold some taxes: 10% on $5,000, 20% on $5,000 to $15,000, and 30% on amounts above $15,000. The withdrawal amount must be added to your income for the year, and a T4RSP slip will be sent to you from your financial institution, showing how much you withdrew and how much taxes they withheld, and the CRA will adjust your income taxes for that year accordingly.

As mentioned in other parts of this book, money from an RRSP can be withdrawn without penalty only to purchase your first home (Home Buyers' Plan) or pay for higher education (Lifelong Learning Plan).

> *Dakarai arrived in Canada in January 2005 from South*
> *Africa. He had $40,000 in assets that he brought with him.*
> *By January 2006, he had gotten a job in his field and earned*
> *$70,000 a year. He bought a home and settled down to raise*
> *a family Dakarai was forty years old when he arrived in*
> *Canada. His financial planner advised him to contribute $500*
> *per month into an RRSP Mutual Fund account invested in a*
> *Canadian Dividend Growth Fund, making an average return*
> *of 7–8% per year. In thirty years, he should have approxi-*
> *mately $566,764 in his RRSP. This will be part of his retire-*
> *ment income.*

Lifelong Learning Plan

This plan, as discussed in Chapter 4, allows you to withdraw money from your own or your spouse's RRSP to finance full-time post-secondary education.

Registered Retirement Income Fund (RRIF)

Once you reach retirement age and need to defund your RRSP, you should convert the RRSP to a RRIF. The maximum age you can have an RRSP is seventy-one. Suppose you simply cash your RRSP without converting all the funds to an RRIF. All that money will be added to your income, this will put you in the highest tax bracket and you will pay close to 50% of it in taxes. However, you are allowed to transfer the entire balance of your RRSP to a RRIF without paying tax. Once in the RRIF, you can make minimum withdrawals each year (monthly) that will be taxable to you at year-end based on your income level, which will probably be lower than the income level you had while you were working. So, if you are still in the highest tax bracket in retirement, you should not be upset that you are paying a lot of your money in income tax as you are in a sweet spot being able to finance your retirement. If you listen to someone who has such an experience, they might tell you that they wished they had not invested in RRSPs. However, they forgot all the tax deductions they got while they were working and how their income is still high in retirement.

In our RRSP illustration above, if Dakarai saved $566,764 in his RRSP and turned age seventy-one this year, he will convert this RRSP to a RRIF and begin making withdrawals of $22,444 in the first year and increasing the amount each year. He will not run out of money until age hundred. No taxes will be withheld on this income, but when he files his income tax, he will add the $22,444 to his other sourced income and would have to pay taxes at the end of the year depending on the tax bracket his overall income falls in.

Registered Disability Savings Plan (RDSP)

This is a plan available to be set up by parents and others to save for long-term care for anyone with a disability. It receives a disability tax credit, and you can make contributions to it up to when the beneficiary turns fifty-nine years old. The government contributes 300%, 200%, or 100% of the amount you invest based on the adjusted family net income of the disabled. The maximum grant per year is $3,500 and $70,000 over the plan's lifetime. These grants stop when the beneficiary turns forty-nine years old. The government also contributes $1,000 per year in Disability Savings Bonds to low-income families (Family incomes of $30,450 or less gets $1,000 and partial amounts above that amount to zero bonds at an income $46,605) if they open an account regardless of whether they contribute or not. The maximum Disability Savings Bonds total over a lifetime is $20,000. The amount you contribute is not deductible from your income tax, but the growth and grants are taxable at withdrawal by the beneficiary.

> *Sherry's parents left her a $200,000 inheritance when they died. Sherry's son Adam has a disability. Now Sherry is concerned about what will happen to her son if she dies. She opened an RDSP account and began to make maximum contributions for him and designated him both as owner and beneficiary. Because Sherry's income is below $30,000 per year, the RDSP gets $3,500 each year from the grant and $1,000 from the bond for a total of $4,500. By the time her son turns forty-nine, he will have received $90,000 in government grants and bonds in his RDSP account.*

Annuity

This is an insurance product. There are different types of annuities, but the essential thing to know is that you give a certain amount of money to the insurance company. Based on your age and insurance calculation, they will pay you a guaranteed amount for life or a certain number of years, regardless of the investment performance. Some are based on the life of two people; some will continue for a specified number of years if the annuitant dies within a specified period from the time of purchase. Rather than converting an RRSP to a RRIF, some people convert it to an annuity at retirement without tax implications. There are several uses for this product, and it is best to consult your insurance advisor if you intend to use these products. Suppose Dakarai with $566,764 in his RRSP, does not have a wife or kids and is not interested in leaving part of his RRSP as an inheritance to anyone. He can buy an annuity with the money. The insurance company will guarantee that they will pay him $30,000 a year for thirty years and if he dies sooner, they will pay a lump sum or nothing at all, depending on the type of annuity.

Employer Pension Plans

There are two types of employer pension plans: defined benefit and defined contribution.

• Defined Benefit Pension Plan

The defined benefit promises that you get a certain fixed amount at retirement, based on your years of employment, your income level, and other pension factors. This is a traditional pension, and nowadays, only government, school boards, and mega-corporations offer them.

• Defined Contribution Pension Plan

These are more common with employers today. In this type of pension, you contribute a certain amount from your payroll. The employer matches that contribution. A plan administrator manages the investment on your behalf according to your risk level and time horizon. Whatever amount is in the pension account when you retire is yours to receive to fund your retirement.

Margaret was a TTC driver, and she got the job right out of college at age twenty-two. She made mandatory contributions to the Defined Benefit Pension Plan. At age fifty-two, they gave her a retirement package that included severance of $95,000 and an annual pension of $55,000 a year indexed to inflation. It means she will always have that income till she dies.

Cathy, her friend from college, also got a job at the same time with Havilah Corporation. She earns good income and contributes the maximum allowed to the Defined Contribution Pension Plan, which is 6% of her income, and her employer also matches her contributions by 100%. So, each year, 12% of Cathy's income is invested for her with the kind of risk she is comfortable with, and when she retires, she will have access to that money to fund her retirement.

Locked-in Retirement Savings Plan (LRSP) and Locked-in Retirement Income Fund (LRIF)

Both RRSPs and Pensions can be transferred from where they are to another institution and, at times, from employer to employer or another institution. If you transfer your pension out from your employer, it must go into an LRSP, and if you are at age seventy-one, it must go into an LRIF. You do not have a choice in these matters. The difference between a Locked-in RSP and a regular RRSP is that you cannot take money out of a locked-in plan. It is like a pension, except under financial hardship rules, like you can't pay rent, or you will lose your home for the missed mortgage payments or in the case of shortened life expectancy if the doctor diagnoses you with a terminal illness. The same thing goes for the Locked-in Retirement Income Fund (LRIF).

> *If Margaret, the TTC Driver above, had decided to leave the TTC when she had only worked for them for ten years and had started her own small business, she would have had the option to transfer out the commuted value of her pension to a financial institution of her choice, and the type of plan it would go in would be a Locked-in Retirement Savings Plan (LRSP), and when she turns seventy-one, she would have to convert it to a Locked-in Retirement Income Fund (LRIF).*

Employee Savings Plan and Stock Options

You should immediately sign up for the maximum amount that your employer offers you. These are plans where the employer gives you stock either as a percentage of income or it's awarded to you. When you buy from your pay, some employers will match it anywhere from 50% to 100%, or the employer issues you stock as part of your bonus or compensation. They can be quite lucrative as it is essentially as if you are making money that you would not have made if you did not choose to take part in this program. An example is, you are working for a company that allows you to contribute up to 6% of your pay to an ESP to buy the corporation's stock, and the company will match it up to 50%. This means if you contribute 6%, they will contribute 3%; if you contribute 0%, they will contribute 0%. Because they buy in bulk and from the treasury, they also get the stocks at a discounted rate, so it's a win for you all the time. Now imagine if they match it 100%.

Some companies give stock options as an incentive to a new hire, a bonus to some employees, and part of total compensation for senior employees rather than increased salary or cash bonuses. After one or two years, these stock options will vest (become yours fully). At that point, you must pay income tax on the dollar value of the stocks received because it is considered as income to the employee. Depending on how the stocks are doing, it might be wise to liquidate them, pay the taxes, open a TFSA with a discount brokerage, and buy the same stocks if you like your corporation. Many Canadians have become millionaires by working for companies where they get stock options, and the company's stock went through the roof. Notable examples are employees of Nortel, Research in Motion (Blackberry), and Shopify.

> *Joshua, a computer whiz, got a job with Shopify in 2015. They give him stock options each year as part of his compensation. Over time, he accumulated 2,000 shares of Shopify. In 2015, one Shopify stock sold for $41, and on November 19, 2021, Shopify stock sold for $2,139. It means, his stock value was now worth $4,278,000.*

Canada Pension Plan

Retirement in Canada is a significant focus of the financial system. The provision of money for retirement is a three-pronged approach. You provide part of the money, the government does their part, and your employer or business provides the last part. I will borrow from a description used by a Canadian financial institution. If all three provide the money, then it's as if you are riding a tricycle. It is well balanced, and there is hardly a chance of a fall or being broke. If you only have two sources, you are riding a bicycle, it is steady, but you must be careful. If you, however, only have one source, it is as though you are riding a unicycle. It takes special skills and a lot of worries to ride it, and you cannot go very far with it. Therefore, it is pertinent that you prepare for retirement as soon as you begin earning income. If you are a salaried worker, your employer will deduct a percentage of your pay, add an equal amount, and pay it to the government as part of your payroll tax deduction each pay cycle. If you are self-employed, you must pay CPP (Canada Pension Plan) dues, both yours as a person and the employer portion. Most business owners who don't declare a lot of income miss out on this. Still, it is highly advisable to ensure that your accountant calculates your percentage of CPP due and pays it to the government each year, so that you have that government source of guaranteed income in retirement. The maximum yearly pensionable earnings for the year 2022 was $64,900. If any business owner can afford to, they should at least pay themselves this maximum amount and its equivalent each year.

My father-in-law lived in Canada from 1967 to 1973. After that, he returned to Nigeria and had a full-fledged career. At age sixty-five, he received his Canada Pension Plan for the period he worked while living here. Now he receives that money monthly compared to his pension situation in Nigeria; he is glad he worked and paid into the CPP.

Old Age Security (OAS) and Guaranteed Income Supplement (GIS)

When you are sixty-five years or older, you are also eligible for Old Age Security payments. It depends on your legal status in Canada, and you must have lived in Canada for ten years after age eighteen. If you are not residing in Canada when you are sixty-five or older, you must have lived as a Canadian citizen in Canada for twenty years to be eligible. Other types of Old Age Security payments include the GIS (Guaranteed Income Supplement), given to very low-income seniors as a non-taxable benefit and an allowance given to spouses of OAS pension payment recipients. In 2022, the maximum monthly payment of OAS was $618.45. For GIS, it is $935.72 for a single person or $583.20 for a married person. This GIS is based on total income and equals zero when your annual income exceeds $19,656 for individuals and $25,968 for married folks. Although, as you can see, these pension figures are designed to ensure that seniors don't become destitute, it is not enough to live the Canadian dream you desire. Be sure that you do all that you can while employed to ensure that these are not your only source of income in retirement.

I have an aunt who studied and worked in Canada in her twenties to early thirties and moved back to Nigeria. She returned as a widow in her sixties and worked a few more years. Finally, at sixty-five, she stopped working. She began receiving the CPP, and because her income was low, she also got the OAS, and since her income was still low, she also got the GIS. Now she can live a decent life and pay her expenses though she is a widow with not much of a pension.

Test Your Knowledge of This Chapter:

1. What are the two major benefits of an RRSP?

2. What are the good ways for you to receive your RRSP money in retirement?

3. What plans exist to save for a child with disability and how much does the government contribute over the life of the plan?

4. What two kinds of pension plans do we have in Canada?

5. What should you do if you get offered an employee savings plan or stock option and why?

6. Is the Canada Pension Plan (CPP) and the Old Age Security (OAS) income enough to finance the lifestyle you desire in retirement?

Chapter 6:

TAXES AND CHARITABLE GIVING

In Canada, we have both Federal and Provincial Income Taxes, the Goods and Service Tax (GST), the Provincial Sales Tax (PST) and the Harmonized Sales Tax (HST).

Income Tax

Income tax is the amount of taxes that the government charges you on your employment income and it is done through your employer. Your employer is required to deduct both the Federal and Provincial Taxes from your pay and send it to the Canadian revenue agency (on your behalf). The deductions your employer is mandated to deduct from your income are Federal and Provincial Taxes, Canada Pension Plan contributions, and Employment Insurance. In addition, depending on your employer, you might have other deductions like Union Dues, Employee Pension Plan deductions, Group RRSP deductions, Group Benefits (Health and Dental), Life Insurance, Employee Share Ownership Plan deductions, and other deductions specific to your employer. If you are self-employed through your business and pay yourself a salary, you must register for the Employment Insurance (EI) program, this program kicks in after 12 months of registering and provides 55% of your earnings up to an annual maximum if you need time off to care for yourself, your children or other family members.

If you earn $60,000 a year without any tax deductions, your biweekly take-home pay would be $2,307.69. However, in Ontario, by just deducting the mandatory deductions of Federal and Provincial Taxes, Employment Insurance, and the Canada Pension Plan, the amount becomes $1,756.42 biweekly. Depending on what else your employer deducts, your take-home pay may be $1,600. Therefore, it is important that you wait for a few months after you get a new job before you start spending your increased salary. Then, get past the customary three-month probation period to know exactly how much your consistent take-home pay is after you qualify and sign up for benefits and other perks your employer offers.

Goods and Service Tax (GST), Provincial Sales Tax (PST) and Harmonized Sales Tax (HST)

This is the tax charged every time you purchase a good or service. Unlike most countries, this amount is not included in the price quoted to you or displayed on the item you are buying. Instead, this amount is added when its time to make a payment, so be careful to have sufficient funds for your purchase. Some provinces charge only the GST on sales of goods and services, Some charge both the GST and PST separately while others charge the HST which is a combination of both. Alberta, North West Territories, Nunavut and Yukon are the only provinces with just a 5% GST and no PST. A GST of 5% is charged in Manitoba, British Columbia, Quebec and Saskatchewan. A PST of 7% is charged in British Columbia and Manitoba while Quebec charges a QST of 9.975% and Saskatchewan charges 6%. An HST of 13% is charged in Ontario and 15% is charged in New Brunswick, Prince Edward Island, Newfoundland and Labrador and Nova Scotia. The government sends a GST/HST refund check to low-income earners every quarter. This is another reason it is important to file an income tax return even if you do not have any income. Zero income earners also qualify for the GST/HST return checks because the government assumes you must have spent some money buying goods and services in the country. The minimum age to qualify for GST/HST is nineteen. It is based on your previous year's income. There is a minimum to a maximum amount for a single person, another for a couple, and a fixed amount per child.

Businesses that charge GST/HST on their goods and services are merely collecting the amount on behalf of the Canada Revenue Agency (CRA) and must remit the money to them regularly. To charge GST/HST, you must have a CRA GST/HST number. In addition, if your service income in a year is expected to be above $30,000, you must charge GST/HST for the work or service you offer.

If you purchase clothes from a store in Ontario and the displayed price is $50, that is not the amount the cashier charges you at check out. You end up paying $56.50 because the HST is 13% in Ontario; this rate is different from province to province. While the amount is not so large on a $50 item, imagine buying a $10,000 item, and you thought all you had to pay was the displayed price. Instead, they add an extra $1,300 to your bill. It could be quite significant if you were not expecting it.

Income Tax Filing

Everyone must file an income tax return by April 30 of the following year. If you are patient and know what you are doing, you can file it yourself or go to a tax filing service and pay a minimal fee for someone to do it for you. If you have a lot of tax forms and think you might have better opportunities of paying fewer taxes, you can consider using an accountant. Here is what you need to know. Your employer deducts taxes from your pay based on your income level. The higher you make, the more you pay. There is a tax bracket that all income falls in; so, employers use this tax bracket to determine how much taxes to withhold from your pay. But they do not have a way of knowing your situation and what tax deductions or exemptions you are eligible for. This is the reason why each employer is required to send you a T4 slip for your last year's income before the end of February every year. This T4 slip shows how much income you made and how much income tax and other deductions were on that income. You then file your income tax return using the T4 as well as other things that might make you eligible for tax breaks. The Canada Revenue Agency (CRA) analyzes it and issues you a refund or requests that you pay more taxes. Examples of deductible things on your income include charitable contributions, school fees, drug expenses, and childcare expenses. You must declare to CRA if you have other sources of income, including other employment income, capital gains on things bought and sold, dividends, and interest income. If you work as a contractor, the business might issue you a

T4A depending on the type of contract worker you are. There will be no tax deductions, so you will be responsible for filing and paying your taxes directly. If you owe CRA, please pay it off as soon as possible, even if you must take a loan, as CRA charges a 5% late filing fee and 1% penalty per month for a maximum of 12 months in 2022.

> *Tobi and Kemi are a young married couple who moved to Canada in 2016. They both got jobs in the same year. Tobi's job was as a business analyst on contract with Telus, and Kemi got employment with Royal Bank as a project manager. At the end of the year. Tobi earned $30,000 as a contractor and did not get any tax documents. Kemi got a T4 showing she earned $40,000 and paid taxes of about $9,000. When he files his income tax return, Tobi will have to pay taxes, and Kemi might get a refund based on her RSP contributions and donation receipt.*

Tax Avoidance

Two things are guaranteed when you live in Canada they are-death and taxes, CRA has however provided a way of escape for those who know, but they can't help you with death. Tax avoidance is legal in Canada. A good financial planner or an accountant can guide you on how to structure your finances in such a way as to avoid paying taxes or paying a large amount of taxes doing different things like contributing money to your RSP or spousal RSP, buying certain types of insurance, borrowing money to invest rather than using your own funds, and many other strategies.

> *In the example of Tobi earning $30,000 from contract work, if he files his tax return with just that information, he will be required to pay a lot of taxes. However, if he contributes about $5,000 to an RRSP, the amount of tax he will be required to pay is reduced dramatically. He has therefore avoided paying higher income taxes.*

Tax Evasion

This is illegal. You must pay taxes on any taxable income that can't be legally avoided. So, beware of tax schemes and anything done purely to evade taxes. Different people and organizations offer tax schemes where you invest some amount of money and get a huge tax deduction. These companies or individuals will earn a high commission for selling it to you. They are usually very sleek and do presentations that seem legit. Please beware of them and check with the CRA if you come across such people. At times, these are offshore investments.

What if an employment agency paid Tobi $30,000, yet did not send him any CRA forms, and he decides not to file that income on his tax return or decides not to file a return at all? He has evaded paying tax, and that is a criminal offense.

Charitable Giving

Whatever seeds you sow in life usually come back to you in multiples of what you have planted. That includes money, kind words, friendship, et cetera. By following this ancient principle, many have attained great wealth in life, which they believe came to them because of their generosity. Most western societies have allowed the creation of charitable entities in their countries, and any taxpayer who donates to those entities is exempt from taxes on the portion of their income that they have donated.

The two major religions in the world, Christianity, and Islam, encourage members to practice the principle of giving. In the Christian faith, part of it is the giving of tithes or 10% of your income to God's house, to widows, orphans and the giving of alms to help the poor. In the Muslim faith, Zakat is giving 2.5% of your wealth to the poor in each lunar year if you qualify. These practices help us think of others and not just ourselves and follow the life principle of sowing and reaping.

Benjamin gave $5,000 to his church in 2019, and his annual income was $50,000. He works for AtlasMedic Group, an equipment manufacturer; therefore, taxes are deducted from his income. He received a donation receipt from the church (a charitable entity) and added it to the things he filed on his income tax. By doing this, he received a tax refund of close to $1,967.78 for that portion of his tax filing. It means that the government is encouraging him to support charities and give to causes that are meaningful to him. Remember, the government cannot solve all societal issues, and most charities do something to help. A tax refund for giving to a charity is not the government giving you money; it is the government taxing you less on your income than they would have loved to, because you did something outside of yourself; so, there is no reason that you should not file your donation slip when doing your income tax return. Most wealthy individuals and business owners use these charitable tax credits as a way to plan their estates. While that is not within the scope of this book, it suffices to say that when a wealthy person donates $10,000,000 to a charity in the form of company shares/stocks or other asset, they may end up being in a better position financially from a tax standpoint than they would have been if they did not make the donation. When you have money, it is important to have a good accountant to guide you on various ways to keep more of your money.

Test Your Knowledge of This Chapter:

1. What two things will happen to you for as long as you are in Canada?

2. What happens to the tax you pay as your income increases?

3. What is tax avoidance and what is tax evasion? Are they both illegal?

4. When should you file your income taxes? By what date?

5. Why should you donate to a charity?

Chapter 7:

INSURANCE

I disliked insurance when I was much younger and did not really know why. A lot of rhetoric makes you feel insurance companies are there to take your money for no reason. You probably won't have a claim, and if you do, they won't pay. Now I know better, while insurance adjusters are stern, they just want to make sure they are only paying necessary claims. There are different types of insurance, ranging from life insurance to debt insurance, car insurance, sickness, accident, and so on. In life, insurance always exists; it is just a question of who is carrying the risk. Insurance is to protect you from a risk that can happen. So, you either self-insure and bear the risk and consequence, or you transfer that risk to an insurance company.

Life Insurance.

Lets look at life insurance. The risk is that one day you might die. Being self-insured says that my assets are sufficient to cover my liability and provide for my loved ones when I die. If you buy insurance, you are transferring that risk to a company. They will assume the risk and pay you an agreed-upon amount when the event occurs, in turn you pay them a monthly or annual premium in exchange for that guarantee. The insurance company can afford to make the payment because they insure many people and by doing so pool the risk. According to probability and actuarial calculations, they know only a certain number of people will succumb to the risk in a shorter period. The same is the case for all other types of insurance. Interestingly, the government has mandated that all drivers have car insurance, and we all do, but other types of insurance are not mandated. It is not uncommon to find people paying $200 per month for car insurance (the risk of having an accident) and $0 for insurance on their life (the risk of dying).

There are two main types of life insurance: Term life and Whole/Universal life.

Term Life

This is a cheap form of insurance that covers a certain value for a specific period, like ten or twenty years. Many advisors market this kind and recommend you buy it for its price and invest the difference you would pay if you had whole life insurance. This is good theoretically but can be difficult because life happens, and you might cancel the investment.

> *Kojo and Efua have two little daughters and own their own home. They had very little disposable cash but did not want to risk not having insurance. So, they both purchased a term life insurance policy for $500,000 to cover them for twenty years. They hope that if anything happens to either of them, the $500,000 will pay off the mortgage on the house, and if nothing happens, they would pay off the mortgage themselves, so there would be no risk to either partner if one spouse dies within twenty years.*

Whole or Universal Life

This is a more expensive type of insurance, and it covers you for your entire life for the value of the policy. It has a life insurance component and an investment or cash component, which can be a source of tax-free retirement income or used to pay premiums in the future. It is better and cheaper to buy insurance when you are young and have no health issues, and once you are covered, you remain covered. This is probably the most important thing to know because some people buy term insurance for twenty years in their thirties. It expires in their late fifties, by which time they have one health issue or the other that makes the premium on a new policy very high; so, be careful when making insurance decisions. You might be better off having both types for different amounts. Many clients use insurance to pass on or create wealth for their heirs. As I mentioned earlier two things you are guaranteed in Canada are death and taxes. As long as you are here, you will one day die, and before that, you will always pay taxes. So, if we are all going to die someday, we might as well ensure that when that time comes, rather than leaving our families in a bad spot, we help them benefit a great deal from it. So, while they are sad that you died, they get consolation in what you did for them.

> *There was a client of mine who was already worth over $90 million. He had an option to invest some new money he just made from a transaction. He would earn 6% tax deferred income on $20 million for ten years and have tax implications from then on. This client was seventy-two years old at the time. He had another proposal from someone else to buy a $10 million insurance policy. He was in good health, and one insurance company agreed to insure him and his younger spouse for $175,000 per month. The insurance would be cancelled if his wife died first. He decided to buy the policy and invest just over $1 million with me. His rationale was that he would be able to give an additional $10 million to his children, who were already wealthy in their own rights. If he had invested the $20 million with me, it would form part of his estate and probate fees and final taxes will apply to the portfolio's growth, but the $10 million insurance will go to his heirs tax-free.*

Different cultures have different concepts of death and dying and discussing one's demise with their children. For some, it's taboo to prepare for it, but others, like this client, know that it's not a question of whether you will die; it is when will you die? He, therefore, maximized what his heirs would get at his death. I have seen countless others who don't talk about insurance or death, and when their parents die, they all have to look for money to pay for their burial and final expenses. Suppose you have an aging parent and do not have a lot of income to cover their final expenses. In that case, it is more cost-effective for you and your siblings to pay a little money monthly toward a guaranteed insurance policy for a small amount to cover the final expense than to wait for death and the need to come up with the money. It costs anywhere from $7,000 to $20,000 to bury someone in Canada, and there are insurance companies that will issue a life insurance policy for such small amounts to seniors, regardless of their health conditions.

Critical Illness (CI) Insurance:

This is insurance that pays out a lump sum should the insured be diagnosed with any of the covered illnesses. Majority of covered illnesses are Cancer or Cardiac related. Our advance medical system makes if possible for a lot of people to survive, so the money from CI insurance can help cover the extra cost of care or replacement of income at the time of sickness. Most Insurers limit the age at which you can own CI insurance. When buying CI make sure your agent explains all what is covered, the coverage amount and at what point payout is done.

There are many different types of insurance in Canada for different purposes a good insurance agent will help you navigate through them to protect you and your family.

Test Your Knowledge of This Chapter:
1. What situations exist where no one is carrying the insurance risk?

2. What's the difference between Term Insurance and Whole Life Insurance?

Chapter 8:

WILLS AND POWERS OF ATTORNEY

There are legal documents that give people a say when they seemingly don't have a say anymore. One is the Will and the other is a Power of Attorney.

Wills

A will is the last testament of a deceased person that lets the executor (the person who fulfills the owner's wishes) know what and how the owner's (testator) assets should be distributed at death. If someone dies without a will, it is called dying intestate. Each province has rules governing how the assets of an intestate person are to be distributed, and most of the time, it is never what the owner would wish. A will can be in the handwriting of the testator (called holographic), or it can be typed up and signed by a notary public. Both are legal. The holographic will can be problematic if there is a dispute. Lawyers charge anywhere from $500 for a simple will to tens of thousands for a complicated one. It is wise to speak to different lawyers, know their expertise, know what you want, and get a sense of the fair price before you create a will. A common problematic example is how a house is divided between spouse and children if it was only owned by the other spouse and no will is in place. To meet the provincial rules of what percentages spouse and children should receive, the house will have to be sold even if the heirs/beneficiaries would rather keep the property. Another situation is, when people are separated from their spouses but were not legally divorced before death, or situations where former spouses were not removed from a will, and they ended up inheriting the assets of the deceased.

Power of Attorney/Living Will

A power of attorney allows you to give someone the authority to make decisions on your behalf while you are still alive but not present or incapacitated. The person (attorney) you have selected will act as though they are you. You can limit what they can do for you, like healthcare decisions and handling finances, or you may give them unlimited power to act on your behalf. It is quite necessary in our age of modern medicine. People must decide if they should be kept on life support machines or not. People with Alzheimer's disease and dementia can live for ten to twenty odd years after being diagnosed. You need to have had a POA before the onset of any of these diseases or an accident. A power of attorney ceases to be in force at the death of the person who granted it.

> *Young Kim is the power of attorney for his brother Alan. Alan got into an accident and was placed on life support. Alan had gotten married to Sue two years before the accident but had not changed his Power of Attorney to his wife. After one month, Young decided to pull the plug against Sue's wishes and because he is the power of attorney, he had legal rights to do so.*

Test Your Knowledge of This Chapter:

1. What is it called if you die without a Will and how will your assets be divided in such a case?

2. What does a Power of Attorney do for you?

Chapter 9:

DEATH AND THE LOTTERY

Most people think that when they die, it's the end, no more obligations and there's nothing else to be done, but this is far from the truth. Just like you have a Will, you can pre- plan for what should happen in case of death.

Death

I'll say it again, death and taxes are the only guarantees in Canada. When a person dies, their legal surviving spouse is entitled to a survivor's pension, which is 60% of the benefit the deceased would have received if they reached age sixty-five or more, and a flat rate plus 37.5% of the pension they are eligible for. Also, the deceased estate gets a lump sum death benefit; the estate must apply for this benefit within sixty days of death. The current maximum benefit is $2,500. The deceased must pay their final taxes, and then they are free to go to heaven, from Revenue Canada's perspective, all jokes aside the executor of the Will, must file a final tax return for the deceased. Final taxes imply that all the deceased assets will be deemed as sold, and gains on them will be taxable, except for anything that has joint ownership with rights of survivorship. Therefore, it is a good tax plan to own some assets jointly with family members. You should consult an accountant to make sure you are not using this to evade taxes.

> *Paulo and his wife Isabela owned their home jointly with rights of survivorship and had separate investment accounts with Royal Bank of Canada $100,000 and $75,000, respectively. Paulo invested $60,000 in his account ten years ago to get this amount. They are both each other's beneficiaries in their wills. Paulo died in 2017, and Isabela filed Paulo's final taxes in 2018. Their home became hers with no tax implication, but he (his executor) must declare a capital gain of $40,000 on the investment with RBC and pay taxes due on it, in his final tax return.*

The Lottery

In Canada, a disproportionately high percentage of people believe they will one day win the lottery, which will be one of the means of financing their retirement. However, analysts have long said that you have more chance of being struck by lightning than winning the lottery! While I do not play the lottery, I have had two clients, who they, or their family member, have won various sums in the lottery. They usually dedicate a certain amount to play every week. In the first one's case, his mum won and gave him $1 million. He quit his job against our financial advice. We had recommended paying off his debt and mortgage, investing and continuing the same lifestyle. He took up golfing very seriously and began to attend major tournaments around the world, got a girlfriend in Europe and frequently travelled to see her, bought expensive golf memorabilia, and eventually finished the money. The second was a single lady who won $1.2 million. She left the funds in cash for a little bit, did not announce to anyone that she had won, kept a low profile on the job, and just lived as though nothing had changed. We invested most of the money, and she updated her will to leave funds for her nephews and nieces. Some of my colleagues have had people win larger sums, and the stories are always the same. Large money comes in, different vices surface, and the client begins to spend money till they finish it. Most say it was the worst thing that happened to them. They now don't know who their true friends are or who simply stuck around for money. Some felt like they lost their path in life. For this reason, my second client maintained a low profile and kept her mouth shut. Either way, it is too long a shot to stake your life and retirement on.

Spending $10 per week for a year works out to be $520 per year. You could invest this in a portfolio that grows yearly and eventually becomes a large amount or in a business investment or real estate investment. Where your returns are more predictable? Also, all lotteries in Canada are licensed and managed by the government agency that handles gambling; so, if gambling is not your thing, I recommend you stay away from it and focus on investing.

Test Your Knowledge of This Chapter:

1. If you own an asset joint with rights of survivorship with someone, what happens to it if you die?

2. How much does the government pay to the family of someone who dies?

3. How realistic is it that the lottery will finance your retirement?

PART 3

Chapter 10:

REAL ESTATE INVESTING

Many immigrants are unfamiliar with real estate investing, especially if they come from countries that do not have highly developed financial markets like the ones in the western world. Moreover, with the rising cost of real estate in Canada, it has become increasingly difficult to own real estate. It, however, is not an impossible feat if you know how and you are willing to go through the process.

Principal Residence

As discussed in chapter 3, this should be your first purchase. Remember, when you are buying your first home, if you are not an extremely high-income earner, the goal should be to buy the best home you can afford and stop renting (wasting money by giving it to the landlord). Purchasing a home builds equity for your next purchase. A simple Google search will provide you with access to mortgage payment calculators on most bank websites and other financial institutions. This will help you determine first, how much your mortgage payment will be, based on your down payment and second, how much you can afford based on your income.

Here is the best way to purchase your home. First, save (preferably by RRSPs and TFSA (Chapter 5 and Chapter 11) 5% of the cost of a home as a down payment to buy it either by yourself, joint with your spouse, family, or friend. Then, once you have the amount you need, contact a mortgage agent or your banker to get a pre-approval or clarify that you will be eligible for a mortgage. Getting a pre-approved mortgage helps you determine the home value you can afford, your down payment, and how much your monthly payments will be. Once you are comfortable with these expenses, plus the cost of property tax and utilities, you can contact a realtor to help you find your house. In Canada, the home seller pays all realtor fees, and your realtor can help search and show you different things to look out for or avoid in a home. You have the right to interview your realtor before you hire them, to ensure that they are not just one to make a quick sale, instead of holding your hands and pointing you in the right direction. Once you choose a home, your realtor will assist you in putting together an offer to the seller. Once accepted, you make a deposit, then they set a closing date. On the closing date or just a little before, you will meet with your lawyer to sign mortgage documents that your bank or mortgage provider would have sent to them. You will need closing costs of between 1.5% to 4% of the price of the house. These include legal fees, land transfer tax, your share of property tax, and other one-time administrative fees. It can really add up, so ensure that you have some money set aside for this. Assuming you have done everything right, you get your keys at closing, and now you are a homeowner.

Let's look at one example of how your mortgage will work with a home purchase if the house's value is $600,000 and your mortgage is $540,000 with $60,000 in equity. Each month, as you make your mortgage payment, a portion of it goes to pay interest to your lender, and a part goes toward the principal. So, most of the time, as your house value goes up from year to year, your mortgage balance decreases.

After a few years, the house value is now $650,000, and your mortgage balance is $520,000. You have $130,000 equity, and you can sell the house or take out the equity by a process called refinancing and buy a better place or part ways with the family member/friend whom you purchased the home with to go and buy your home solo. Use caution when buying a home with someone other than your spouse. You should have a legal document that shows how much you contributed to the purchase and what percentage of ownership/equity each has at the purchase. It will also be helpful if you all determine the minimum time you will hold the property for or how you will share the equity. A good lawyer can help you out with that, and it will clarify what you agreed going in and save you a lot of headaches in the future.

Property Taxes

You pay these to the city where you buy your house. It is based on the square footage of your home and the lot size of your property. Most banks add the amount to your mortgage payments and remit it to the city on your behalf if your down payment for the home purchase is less than 20%. Some cities charge you 1.25% interest per month, plus a late payment charge if you owe property taxes. These can add up quickly, so it is wise not to owe the city. The city always secures the property tax amount as the house cannot change owners without settling the outstanding amount. If you owe property taxes and try to refinance your home, the institution will use part of the funds to pay off any overdue amount.

> *Roselyn bought a Townhouse for $700,000. She made a down payment of $70,000, her mortgage including mortgage insurance premium was for $649,530 at 5% interest rate, and the monthly amount was $3,770. She was shocked when the payment requested by her mortgage lender was $4070. They had added $300 per month for property tax payments because she did not make a 20% down payment; therefore, they pay the property tax to the city on her behalf.*

Buying Residential Rental Properties

When you have enough down payment, usually 10% to 20%, you can purchase a rental property; it can be a condo, a townhouse, a house, a rooming house, or an apartment. You must research it properly, know the demographics of the people who live in the neighbourhood, visit Viewit.ca and Kijiji to confirm the rental price in the area, and ensure that you can cover at least the mortgage payment with the rental income. While it is true that the law somewhat favours tenants, you can protect yourself by doing all the right things. Here are some key areas to consider before becoming a part-time landlord:

- Due to COVID 19 induced wait times at the Landlord and tenant board you should have about 4 to 6 months of your mortgage payment amount in the bank or an overdraft protection of the equivalent, in case you have issues with the tenant.

- Advertise and choose tenants wisely.

- Make sure tenants have proof of income and good character that you can judge in various ways.

- Establish the rental rate as a fixed amount plus utilities to minimize the cost and work you must do.

- Collect the first and last months' rent when they sign the lease.

- Depending on how handy you are, you can buy a newer or older home and find a team of plumbers, handymen, and electricians you can use at a moment's notice.

You make your money work for you by collecting the rents and managing the property. Usually, it takes a few years before the property value appreciates significantly while a tenant is paying down the mortgage. Once you have built enough equity in the property, you can take it out and buy another one. No matter your investment preference, I believe that everyone should own at least one rental property. I know of business owners who've made money all their life and later lost the business close to retirement. They used the rental properties they bought while doing business to finance part of their retirement.

> *I had a client who bought five properties, including his principal residence, during the 1990s' real estate corrections. He and his wife had a very modest income and purchased a home for $240,000 just before interest rates rose to 18%, and most owners could not afford their mortgage payments and were losing their homes. One day, he took a stroll and saw a nice house with a For Sale sign on his street. He called the real estate agent, got the price, went to the bank, and asked if they would give him a mortgage. The bank agreed; he called the agent to ask how much he could rent it for. The realtor gave him an estimated rental rate of $200 higher than the mortgage and property tax amount, so he bought it and rented it out. The following month, he saw another one for sale; he got the price, repeated the process, and rented it out. He did it two more times until his wife's fear of what would happen if the tenants did not pay rent, stopped him from doing it again. I met him sixteen years later, and he had paid the mortgages on those properties down to between $35,000 and $45,000 each. The properties were worth $600,000 each over ten years ago. Today each property is worth about $3.5 million, his income was still in the same range when I met him, and I am sure he would have retired by now.*

There are many ways you can rent your property. One friend rents rooms to students. This can be very lucrative as the rental rate of each room far exceeds the rent for an entire house. Another friend does short term rentals on Airbnb and Vrbo, which takes more of your time, since you must handle bookings and maintain the property more regularly than a long-term rental. Airbnb operators in the right area can make double or close to triple of what a long-term tenant will pay in one month. That is pure income that exceeds any part-time job you can think of.

In today's world, real estate prices have risen in the larger, more metropolitan cities, but there are other areas where the prices are still reasonable. Be innovative when purchasing a rental property. For example, you can buy a home for yourself that has a basement apartment, which you can rent out. Target areas with high demand by renters, such as a university town or an industrial area.

Buying a Commercial Property

Owning a commercial property differs greatly from owning a residential property. Commercial real estate includes malls, shopping centers, apartment buildings, medical buildings, hotels, warehouses, office buildings, et cetera. Some realtors specialize in commercial properties. One of the chief advantages of owning commercial real estate is that a buyer can deduct the value of the commercial loan, mortgage interest, or depreciation in the building's value from the corporation's taxes.

As with any real estate investment, location is the number one thing in commercial real estate and second to it is occupancy. However, you need to first consult an accountant and a realtor who knows about commercial real estate to evaluate the income potential of the property you want to buy. In addition, you need to be aware of any potential developments in the area that might increase your value in the future or any renovations you might be required to make that can attract better tenants.

Consider these factors when buying commercial property:

- Costly repairs can spoil what looks like a good investment, so check this carefully and consider having a professional look at it.

- Determine the taxes on the property and how much the bank will be willing to finance as a commercial loan so that you know how much down payment you require.

- Most properties are leased as four walls, and the tenant can renovate them to suit their purpose. This can provide a sweet spot for a landlord with A-1 tenants who would not want to change locations.

- Leases can be for a five year term or more, with the option to renew. Unlike residential properties, the amount paid by tenants is not subject to governmental restrictions like the rate of rent increase. Everything is negotiated between the tenant and landlord. While it is common to have five-year terms on a lease, you can refuse to renew if it does not serve your purposes.

- You usually need a larger down payment of 20% to 30%, and there may also be a limit on the amount of loan you qualify for with the lenders. When buying one, it is best to use an accountant knowledgeable about commercial properties.

- They grade tenants in these properties based on their type of business. So, for example, a Tim Hortons will be a stronger tenant than a flower shop in your building.

Shelley and Maggie are sisters; they pooled their resources and bought a building with four apartments on the first and second floors and two retail shops on the main floor. They both live in one apartment each and rent out the two apartments and the two retail spaces. The tenants pay their utilities, and the two businesses occupying the stores pay part of the maintenance and property tax. They have a very positive cash flow from this property and are looking to buy more.

Buying New Build Condos

It takes three to five years to build a new condo, and many of them are springing up in major cities in Canada. Investors can pre-purchase these condos by putting down the required amount as a down payment, usually 10% to 15% depending on the builder. By the time they complete most condos, the value will have appreciated much more than when you bought it. Investors can then turn around and flip this condo before closing and cash in their profit.

> *Tom had $35,000 in his savings account and found a new condo building downtown in 2006, close to the Waterfront and in a nice area. He made a down payment of $35,000 for one unit and then borrowed another $35,000 from his LOC for another unit. The purchase price for the condos at the time was $350,000. When the condos were ready in 2009, they sold for $444,000. He sold one, made a profit of $144,000 before fees and taxes and closed on the other. Because many condo builders need a percentage of the condos sold before getting financing to build from the bank, they often partner with realtors who have high net worth clients to sell them a few of these condos.*
>
> *In 2008, we had a client who was a chief executive at a telecoms company, he bought twenty-two units of a downtown condo with no intention of closing on any of them. He simply cashed his investments and made the down payments required on twenty-two of them, and when they were ready, his realtor sold them for him. He made a handsome profit.*

Buying a House on Acres of Land

If you are purchasing a property on over ten acres of land or more, lenders calculate the appraisal of the property using just ten acres of land value. As a result, you will need to have a very high down payment to make the lenders comfortable loaning you money, which means you are technically using your funds for the land purchase. Some people have been able to buy land in areas that they thought were remote, and fifteen to twenty years later, development reaches their property and greatly increases its value.

> *Martin lived in Toronto as a teenager and played golf in Whitby Ontario, off a major road. He bought a three-bedroom house on twenty acres of land in the area in 1987 for $80,000. By 2020, Highway 7 and 407 extended nearby, and the property value was now worth over $1.9 million. He was able to apply to the city and sever the property into twenty one-acre lots, and he is developing a design-build estate with nineteen homes.*

Buying and Selling Land

I only had a few clients who did this type of real estate investing, but it can be quite a lucrative venture. Most cities designate land use, so it is a bit risky. You usually need to have cash that you are willing to park for a very long time. Banks don't lend you money to buy land, so most people inherit land or use savings to buy it.

An old client of mine lived in Toronto in the '70s and foresaw that the city would grow, and he went as far out of Toronto as possible to buy land. When he purchased the land, it was only $12,000 per acre, so he bought 240 acres. When I met him forty years later, he was selling the land in Richmond Hill which had now become a major city at $450,000 per acre.

Another of my client's dad bought a cottage in Saskatchewan. They used to go there as kids, and they hated it because it was far out of town. After his father died, neither he nor his siblings visited the place, but thankfully, they did not sell it. One day, he received a call from an oil company who wanted to buy rights to mine oil on the property as they had tested and believed it had oil. He hung up several times on them as he thought it was a hoax. When he finally realized it was real and made a deal with them, they struck oil, and now he, his mother, and two siblings share a 25% royalty on the oil mined on that property. It was that income that made him become my client. He got approximately $225,000 every quarter as his one-quarter share in royalties.

However, it's not all as rosy as these two cases. I had another client who bought land in Ajax in the '70s when most of the development was in downtown Toronto. Sometime in the '90s, he got a letter from the city that they were exercising eminent domain (taking over the land) as it was the ideal site of a power station, and they paid him the city value of the land, not what it was worth in the market.

Test Your Knowledge of This Chapter:

1. What is the minimum number of properties you should aspire to own?

2. Can you work as a part-time landlord? If so, when will you see the full result?

3. What's the difference between residential real estate and commercial real estate?

4. If you saw a piece of land that you, like how will you buy it?

Chapter 11:

THE INVESTMENT LANDSCAPE

Several investment vehicles in the market function differently and are used to fulfill different needs. Therefore, it is essential to know what they are and what they do.

GICs (Guaranteed Investment Certificates)

GICs are investments that are completely guaranteed by the institution that sells it. They are usually issued by banks and trust companies. The institution guarantees the principal amount and a specific interest rate for a specified period from seven days to five years. They are not only guaranteed by the issuing trust company but also guaranteed by the CDIC (Canadian Deposit Insurance Corporation), which is a government agency that insures deposits at the banks, up to a maximum of $100,000 per issuer. This guarantee is for when or if the issuer goes bankrupt, the CDIC will pay the owner back. Most banks own more than one trust company or issuer to cover more than $100,000 in different issuers, at $100,000 per issuer.

An example of this is the Bank of Montreal; they have three issuers or trust companies: Bank of Montreal, Bank of Montreal Mortgage Corporation, and Bank of Montreal Trust Company. These are three separate issuers, and by investing in GICs through them, you can be covered or guaranteed for up to $100,000 each. However, these guarantees do not cover GICs over five years or GICs denominated in US dollars. The names used for similar products worldwide are Certificates of Deposit (CD), Fixed Deposits, and Bank Deposits.

Mrs. Greenberg had $300,000 to invest and wanted the funds guaranteed in case the bank went bankrupt. So, she bought $100,000 each in three different issuers at the Bank of Montreal. If she had $500,000, she could invest the $300,000 in all the issuers at the Bank of Montreal and the remaining $200,000 at two different issuers at TD Canada Trust, TD Mortgage Corporation, and TD Investment Corporation.

While GIC is guaranteed, you should consider that if the return you are getting on the investment is lower than the inflation rate, you are technically losing money or the purchasing power of the money you invested. For instance, if you invest $1,000 at 1% and inflation is at 3%, then the value of the $1,000 is now $970 and you made an interest of $10; therefore, your $1,000 is now worth $980.

Mutual Funds

These are investments sold by licensed representatives, independents, and those working for banks, investment houses, brokerages, et cetera. For anyone to sell mutual funds, they must first pass the Canadian Securities Institute (CSI) IFIC (Investment Fundamentals Course) and be registered/licensed by the MFDA (Mutual Fund Dealers Association).

How a Mutual Fund Works

A fund company hires a fund/portfolio manager and sets a mandate or parameters for which to invest (The fund objective), and gives the manager seed capital to start investing accordingly. The manager buys a basket (group) of investments like stocks, bonds, ETFs, real estate, overseas stocks, et cetera according to the objective. Then, the fund company engages in marketing efforts and sells this packaged portfolio, now called a mutual fund, to investors. When you purchase, you will be buying units of the fund, thereby giving the fund company more money to purchase more investments in the basket. The fund company charges a fee for managing the investment portfolio (basket). The fee charged is known as the MER or management expense ratio, and other fees may also apply. The purchaser can buy a DSC (Deferred Sales Charge) fund, a front-load, low-load, or no-load fund. As the names suggest, with a DSC fund, you don't pay a purchase fee to the agent who sold it to you when you bought it. However, the company whose fund was sold will still pay a commission to the adviser and then put a note on the investment, that you have to stay invested in it for a specific period. Otherwise, the company will recoup, the commission they paid from you when you sell it in a short period. The time is usually five years; some fund companies go up to eight years. The fees charged to redeem or get out are usually on a declining scale, with some starting as high as 6%; because the amounts can be steep, you must verify if the fee exists when buying from your agent. The front-load means paying an upfront commission to the sales agent when buying the fund. The low load means the fees are smaller and for a shorter period, and the no-load, which the banks usually sell, means you do not pay any commission to buy or sell the fund; therefore, you are not restricted. The fact that a fund has a load or no-load does not change the requirement to pay an MER (Management Expense Ratio). They calculate this fee each day and charge it to the fund portfolio monthly before any returns are calculated; regardless of whether the mutual fund makes a positive or negative return, it still gets charged. A good way to understand it is, if your fund earns a return of 6% and the MER is 2%, it means the fund made an 8% return before expenses. Therefore, the portfolio mustn't make negative returns for an extended period as you are paying fees to someone to lose money for you. Mutual funds in some countries are called Unit Trusts.

Mrs. Parker had a mutual fund at an independent mutual fund company with a Deferred Sales Charge. She was upset with the advisor and wanted to immediately transfer her funds to me. On reaching out to the fund company, I found she had a Deferred Sales Charge of 5% on her funds and had to wait four more years before it expired, and she could transfer or take out her fund with no penalty. We did not transfer the funds because of the fee, and she was quite upset because she was not aware she had them.

The new CRM 3 (Client Relationship Model number 3) regulations in the mutual fund industry now make it mandatory that advisors disclose all fees and compensation they receive in connection with any transaction of each client.

> *Mr. Roeper had an emergency and needed to sell his mutual fund. They were in a five-year DSC fund, and it had only been three years. So, he sold it and paid a DSC of 2% to the fund company.*

As of June 1st 2022; Regulators have banned the sales of DSC funds in Canada.

Segregated Funds

These are like mutual funds, except that they have an insurance component. A Segregated fund guarantees that a portion, usually 70% to 75% of the invested amount, is guaranteed, regardless of market performance, and this minimum guaranteed amount is resettable every one to five years. It also offers creditor protection from the investment, so it is ideal for small business owners who could easily get into a situation where a creditor comes after their assets; because a segregated fund is considered an insurance product, and insurance is exempt from creditors. The guaranteed component and insurance element make segregated funds have a much higher management expense ratio (MER) than mutual funds. Also, the higher the guaranteed component and the frequency to reset it, the higher the fund's management expense ratio.

> *Mr. Krees, a merchant in the clothing business, had invested solely in Seg Funds. But unfortunately, he overextended himself, and during the 2001 market correction, he lost his business. The creditors came after him and took all the business assets, his RRSPs, and savings—all that he had. However, they could not touch his Seg Funds as it offers creditor protection, which saved him from losing everything.*
>
> *Ms. Smith invested $30,000 in Seg Funds in 2002, just after the tech bubble burst. The guaranteed amount was $22,500. The portfolio grew each year, and so did the guaranteed amount. In 2006, she reset the portfolio that had become $45,000, and she reset the guarantee, which was now $33,750. This means that no matter how bad the market ever gets, she will never have a loss beyond $33,750, which is higher than the original amount she invested back in 2002. When the markets crashed again in 2008, she did not lose beyond $33,750.*

Index or Indices

The index is the benchmark or indices of a particular thing. A stock market index is a collection or portfolio of the top stocks in that market. For example, the S&P TSX index (Standard and Poor Toronto Stock Exchange Index) is a portfolio of the top 250 stocks on the Toronto stock exchange, and they represent the Canadian market. Similarly, the DJIA (Dow Jones Industrial Average) has thirty of the largest stocks traded in the US and represents the US market. The Nasdaq tracks 3,300 stocks listed on its exchange, while the S&P

500 tracks 500 top stocks in the US. In each country, the best-traded stocks are grouped together and tracked daily. In Tokyo, Japan it is called the Nikkei, Hang Seng in Hong Kong, FTSE in London, UK to mention a few. With the advent of technology and sophisticated systems, there is an index for almost any thing or group you can imagine: We have the gold index, oil index, precious metals index, bank index, and more. Some indexes are the largest or most active stocks in the market, while others are based on measurements in a particular field, like an agricultural index or precious metals like the gold index.

> *Rose bought the Canadian index fund and the US index fund in her RRSP account with one of the mutual fund companies. Over time, the portfolio returns was similar to the S&P TSX Index and the S&P 500 US index. The Management Expense Ratio on the funds are about1.15%, and she has done very well over the last ten years.*

Exchange-Traded Funds (ETF)

An exchange-traded fund is a fund that tracks or mirror-images a specific index; they are bought and sold on the stock exchange, usually without any commissions. Because they merely track an index, the management company charges extremely low fees, and you can only buy these ETFs in a brokerage or discount brokerage account. In the last fifteen years, they have become highly sought after, as investors have noticed that most mutual fund managers can not beat the index consistently. Why should you pay high fees for someone to try to beat the index when you can pay a very nominal fee to be in the index? There is a plethora of ETFs available in the market as there are several indexes. While some ETFs track the index, others are a variant of the same index. This means, the managers use options and derivatives on the index such that you can have an S&P TSX inverse ETF (you will earn a return that is the exact opposite of what the S&P TSX does) or Nasdaq double ETF (which means you will get a return that is double whatever the Nasdaq does). Some ETFs give you access to invest in agricultural produce without buying an agriculture stock, and the list goes on. Most things about life have measurements, and you will probably find an ETF that tracks it. Everything is available, even ETFs that track climate change and a Bitcoin ETF.

Mr. Fernando buys the Canadian Banks' ETFs. This ETF tracks the performance of tier-one Canadian banks, and he has done extremely well over the last fifteen years. He says if we only have six major banks, with all the regulations they are subject to, these banks will continue to make money. He has not been wrong. The ETF has a steady dividend and grows steadily.

Stocks (Shares)

These are actual ownership in a part of a corporation. When you buy a stock or shares, you become part-owner of the corporation and based on the outstanding shares, the number of shares you own is your part of the corporation. You get one vote per share, and if the company pays dividends, you get the amount distributed per share that you invested. Shares or stocks become available to the public when the owners of the corporation do an IPO or initial public offering, based on the share capital or value of the corporation. After this event, every time you buy the shares of that corporation, you must do it on the stock market by dealing with other owners through a brokerage or discount brokerage firm. If the corporation is doing well, the share value goes up, and the share owner can get some of the corporation's profit if the corporation pays a dividend (this is a portion of the corporation's profit broken down into an amount that each share of the company earned. It is not mandatory for the company to issue dividends). Conversely, if the corporation is doing poorly, the shares or stocks decline. Most of the time, news about a company makes the value go up or down. As you guessed, good news will lead to a rise in share value, and bad news will cause a decline. This can be interesting because, at times, a company's fundamentals have not changed (meaning it might still be profitable, have good management, good revenue, cash flow, etc.). Still, a competitor's demise and bad press can negatively impact it. A wise investor will buy such a company because once the news and bad press die down, the share value will go back up.

A certain multi-millionaire owned a fund company and got extremely bad press in the early 2000s about his company going bust. Most people rushed to withdraw all their investments with the fund company. The shares became depressed, and shares of similar companies followed suit as there were speculations that things were bad in the investment world. So, he simply went out and bought almost 10% of a competitor's shares. By the time the news hit the press that he was not going bankrupt but rather now owned almost 10% of a competitor. Everything stabilized, the shares went up in value for both corporations, and he became a billionaire.

An easy way to begin trading in shares is to open a discount brokerage account. You can do this at most banks, and we have a few independent brokerages as well. You can open a TFSA (Tax Free Savings Account), RRSP (Registered Retirement Savings Plan), or just a cash account. Once you deposit money in it, you are ready to trade.

There are many ways you can decide on which stock to buy. The first thing you need to decide is how much percentage gain or percentage loss you would be willing to accept and what type of portfolio you will have. Next, determine whether it will be all high-volatile stocks, like technology stocks, which could sell for $10 per share today and could be $100 per share in one year, if they become very hot, like Spotify, Apple, Meta, or Tesla. or do you want to buy Blue Chip stocks, which are established companies that are steady and pay dividends, like the Banks, Walmart, Heinz, and such. Your portfolio could also be a mix of highly volatile stocks and some Blue-Chip stocks, and even bonds and ETFs. You can list all the items you use in your household, from car insurance to the car you drive, toothpaste, soap, laptop, phones, and TV, and research those companies to see if they trade on the stock market and analyze their stocks. Avoid buying on stock tips because, by the time the information reaches you, it's already known to the market, and the price has adjusted accordingly.

Trading from a stock tip by an insider of an organization on information that is not yet public knowledge is a fraud.

Five Simple Ways to Analyze Stocks:

1. Price Earning (P/E) ratios: A low price-to-earnings ratio indicates the company is undervalued.

2. Earnings Per Share (EPS): A high earnings per share is good; it shows the health of a company.

3. Dividend yield: If a company pays a good dividend, it's an indicator of health, but most high-tech companies do not pay dividends; instead, they use the money for research and development.

4. Charts: You can also use charts. Check the highest and lowest value in one year and, over a more extended period, look at the patterns to see if it is in a recovery mode or a downward trajectory.

5. Once you have taken these steps, buy your stock and monitor the gains or losses according to the parameters you have set for it.

IPO (Initial Public Offerings)

This is when a corporation sells stock or shares its ownership with the investing public. An underwriter uses the earnings of the corporation and the multiples of similar companies in its industry, the outlook of the company, and several other factors in determining the company's value and how much each share should cost. All the money raised during this process goes to the corporation and is used to finance their expansion or research or whatever they choose to do with it. From that day onwards, the shares will trade on the exchange, and individuals can buy and sell them to each other based on the prevailing stock price. They make IPOs available to institutional investors, fund managers, and the like. Many ordinary folks buy stocks at the Initial Public Offering (IPO) stage through brokers. If they are lucky and their discount broker is participating, they can place an order for it. However, institutional traders with millions of dollars get the first dibs on it. While you can evaluate these companies based on their financials for the offering, there is an element of risk, as you cannot predict accurately which direction the stock will go. Many owners and some investment houses already have a stake in the company at prices far lower than offered at the IPO stage.

When Facebook had their IPO (the first time they sold shares in the company to the general public) on May 18, 2012, the share price was $38 per share, which made the value of the newly listed company the same as Royal Bank, the highest valued company in Canada at the time. Most experienced brokers did not buy at that price. However, within weeks of opening and for the next four months, the price declined to less than $18, and investors rushed in at that price. Facebook did not have a clear revenue model, but with time and $16 billion in equity capital, they figured it out. Mark Zuckerberg became an instant billionaire. Some of the earlier investors sold at a loss, but those who stayed invested reaped the rewards as Facebook is around $232 at the time of this writing. If you purchased 100 shares at $38 for $3,800, those shares will be worth $232,000 now. This shows the power of investing, the risks, the temptation to sell when you are down, and the reward to those who stay invested.

A similar stock is Snapchat. It started at $27, traded as low as $5.71, and now trades for $23. Most times, it is a hit-and-miss game with IPOs.

Bonds

A bond is a note or document issued by large borrowers like the federal, provincial, or municipal government, corporation, or government parastatals. It shows that the lender guarantees full repayment of the amount borrowed (face value of the bond) at a specified date (maturity date) and the interest payments (coupon) to be made periodically. Three major rating agencies rate bonds worldwide (Moody, S&P, and Fitch). The rating of bonds shows how strong the bond's issuer is, and consequently, the stronger the issuer, the higher the rating and the lower the interest rate they will offer. Conversely, the weaker the issuer, the lower the rating, the higher the interest rate they must offer. AAA Bonds are the best in the market and they are rated as investment grade while BBB are Junk Bonds and these have the highest interest rates to compensate for the high risk. For example, at the time of writing this book, a country like Canada has a rating of AAA and yields 0.82 on a twenty-year bond, while a country like Nigeria has a B- and yields 10.82% on a twenty-year bond. It means that if the government of Canada wants to build infrastructure, a new highway around the country, and wants to borrow money from investors to do so, it will cost them about 1% in interest payments, while it will cost the Nigerian government almost 11% in interest payments. The bond market is about 30% bigger than the stock market.

Consider Mr. Benji. He is a retired widower living in Toronto. He only has one son who lives in Alberta and has a good job. Mr. Benji sold his home, and the proceeds along with his other nest egg amounted to $2 million. He needs to pay $3,500 per month to the retirement home and $500 in other expenses every month. So, he bought bonds that yield approximately 2.5% per year or $50,000 a year. This was sufficient to pay for his expenses without considering his other income sources and tax calculations.

Investment Trusts

Earlier, we discussed the corporation and how it has shares. Investment Trusts are companies that have set themselves up in a way that its owners, rather than owning shares, own units of the trust company. The company does not pay any taxes but must distribute 90% or more of its taxable income to the unitholders, who then pay taxes at the individual level. Because of these profit distributions, most trusts have a high yield paid to their unitholders on a quarterly or monthly basis, and like bonds, they can be a source of steady cash flow. The most common types of investment trusts are the Real Estate Investment Trusts (REIT's), most of whom own malls, senior residences, and commercial buildings. The trusts typically have a higher yield than GICs, bonds, or dividends, so they are very attractive to seniors who need income from their investments. The trusts trade on the stock market, just like stocks.

A couple I knew, Mr. and Mrs. D'Souza, owned a rental property for years. When Mr. D'Souza died, his wife could not keep up with handling the tenants and doing maintenance work, so she sold the property and invested the proceeds after fees and taxes of $700,000 in a real estate investment trust with a yield of 6.6% per annum. As a result, Mrs. D'Souza gets $46,200 a year, which is sufficient to pay all her expenses, including taxes. She later on decided to bequeath the trust to her only daughter upon her death.

Brokerage

A brokerage is a stock broking company; you deal with a Stockbroker or Investment Advisor, usually with good qualifications and experience with investments. Investments Advisors typically deal with affluent clients and give you advice on what securities to buy and sell in return for a commission on the trades, or they work on a fee-based model, which means they charge you a fixed percentage of the assets they manage for you. Most brokers deal with clients that have upwards of $250,000 to invest. CIBC Wood Gundy, BMO Nesbitt Burns, Canaccord Genuity Group and RBC Wealth Management are some of the brokers in Canada. If we consider investments as a game, many investors are new to the game and do not know how to play it. They therefore need someone to guide them so they can avoid major loss.

> *When Mrs. Perkins lost her husband in 2013, she knew nothing about investing and had received an insurance payment of $5 million. We introduced her to a stockbroker who could invest for her and give her advice and the peace of mind that someone was looking after her portfolio. The advisor charged her a 1.25% management fee. He reviews her account with her once a year and points her in the right direction regarding her tax, insurance, and accounting needs.*

Discount Brokerage

Unlike a full-service broker, a discount brokerage will provide a platform for you to trade in securities without offering any advice, but they provide a very informative research website. Depending on what you are buying and the quantity, they will charge a discounted commission or minimal trading fees ranging from $0 to $50 per trade. Most have the option for you to place a trade online or over the phone with an agent. They can hold your Registered Retirement Savings Plan (RRSP), Tax-Free Savings Account (TFSA), and other investment accounts. This is the classic DIY (Do it yourself) investment platform. All the tools are available to you. You, therefore, need to educate yourself so that you know what you are doing before investing your hard-earned money using a hunch or a tip from a friend who has no clue what they are doing. Quest trade, Qtrade, CIBC Investors Edge, BMO InvestorLine, and TD Waterhouse are some of Canada's discount brokerages. You can buy both Canadian and US stocks on them, keeping your securities in US or Canadian dollars.

At just twenty-two years old, Jaime graduated from the University of Toronto, and his grandfather gave him a gift of $50,000. He had no plans for the money for the next ten years, so he opened a discount brokerage account and began researching and trading stocks. Within three years of trading, he became very good at it, and his portfolio grew to $70,000.

Investment Advice and DIY Investing

There is a lot of chatter out there about do-it-yourself investing and the "huge" savings you can reap by simply learning how to invest online without any professional assistance. Although this can work for some, especially with smaller portfolios, I would advise you to think twice about managing a sizeable investment portfolio without some professional advice.

I had a client who inherited $250,000. She was a sophomore university student in the sciences and did not know anything about investing, so she came to see me. During our client discovery session, I found that both her parents were dead, and she needed income from the money for her living expenses to supplement her work income and pay for university. So, I got her invested in a balanced investment that paid out about 5% in income. She agreed and invested the funds and was fine with it for three years; she graduated and one day in the fourth year, she asked me to withdraw all the funds and place them in a Guaranteed Investments for three years at a rate of 1.25%. I showed her the previous performance of the investment and how she had paid for school and still not lost her principal. Her age and her risk tolerance were still the same. But she insisted, and we did the transfer.

When I asked her why she had been adamant about the decision, she informed me that her older brother had told her to do it. I asked her if her brother was an investment adviser; she responded that he wasn't but follows the market. Think of this. He probably spends a good ten hours working his job each day and a few hours watching investment news in his spare time and makes investment decisions based on what he might have seen on television or the internet. I spend ten hours of my day on investments and a few hours on other things. The odds are stacked against him. Needless to say, my client stayed in this locked GIC at 1.25% for three years, while her former portfolio returned an 8% average in those three years.

Financial Plans

A financial planner creates financial plans for clients. They look at the client's overall financial position from an investment angle, debt, taxes, legal, insurance, and estate perspective. They typically will interview the client to get a sense of what they are currently doing and what they would like to achieve in the midterm and long term. Once they figure this out, they make recommendations on how to go about achieving the set goals most cost-effectively. Most certified financial planners specialize in two or three areas and do their best to align client goals with the actions they take. Some fee-based financial planners get compensated by the clients paying for them to do a comprehensive plan, which they will review annually. Other financial planners create plans and then sell their clients investments or insurance to meet those goals and get compensated by the company whose products they sell. Then, some financial planners are a hybrid of both systems. You must know how your financial planner works, and you can do that by interviewing them. Some planners work for institutions like the bank and deal with bank clients, and independent financial planners work for themselves and represent several financial institutions and insurance companies.

I met with a couple, the Dohertys. After an hour-long session of going through the financial planning process, I discovered they own their home, $200,000 in RRSPs, and $80,000 in a Non-Registered Investment account. They also have $24,000 in a savings account and $25,000 in RESPs. Mrs. Doherty wanted to retire in five years, while Mr. Doherty wanted to retire in ten years. They both have a good income of $150,000 and $170,000, respectively. Mrs. Doherty had a work pension that would pay her 60% of her employment income, and she would be eligible for it in five years.

Mr. Doherty thought they did not have enough money to retire and planned to work for ten more years. They have two daughters: one is a junior accountant and the other is in third year of university. They desired to leave the children a very good inheritance but only have $200,000 in life insurance. When I reviewed their income and expense, they had $1,900 cash flow or income left after paying all expenses, and they had just been accumulating it in the savings account for a rainy day. They feel that if their children decide to pursue a master's degree, they would like to be able to help with the tuition. Mr. Doherty was fifty-seven, and Mrs. Doherty was fifty years old. They have a simple life and go on a vacation once a year and would like to do a cruise to different parts of the world when they retire. They would also like to coach or mentor young boys and girls in the community.

As a financial planner, the questions I asked brought out all the above information, and the following things occurred to me. The Dohertys have almost $100,000 in savings and a non-registered account earning interest income, but they don't have a tax-free savings account. They have an excellent cash flow which they can use to support an insurance payment but have only $200,000 in life insurance. They don't have a critical illness or disability insurance policy, and they have not maximized their RRSP contributions in the last few years. With a bit of adjustment, they can both retire in five years and have enough money to meet their expenses. Then, they can join the Boys and Girls Club as mentors this year to get a feel for mentoring once every two weeks.

The planner uses their knowledge and experience to look for the best way for the clients to do things, and while we cannot address all the issues in one meeting, the planner will work with the client such that they meet all the needs over time.

Insurance Advisor

The insurance advisor is usually a representative of one or more insurance companies and sells various insurance products like life, disability, and critical illness plans. In contrast, others do general liabilities like home and auto insurance or both. They are primarily self-employed; others work for a company and earn a fixed salary and commission.

> *Consider a lady named Venise. She called an insurance broker to see if she could get a better rate for her upcoming car insurance renewal. He takes her information, shops around for the best rate, and gets her a quote of $2,200 a year, which is $400 cheaper than her current rate of $2,600. She was happy with the quote and went to meet with him, to sign the agreement. In the meeting he questions her about her critical illness and life insurance coverage and finds she only has a group life insurance at work. She is forty-six years old with no health issues; he asks her what would happen to her if she developed health problems in the future and the possibility of losing her job or changing employers. She immediately saw the benefit of having her own personal insurance, and because she was a single mum with a ten-year-old child, she did not want to risk not having insurance if something happened to her. So, he sold her a Universal Life Policy of $300,000, it has an insurance and investment component, and she could afford the premium of $350 per month.*

Tax-Free Savings Account (TFSA)

This account is for everything else in life. Though it is called a Tax- Free Savings Account, that name is a bit misleading. A better name for understanding it is a Tax-Free Investment Account. You can have several types of investments ranging from ordinary savings to GICs, stocks, and mutual funds. The concept is that whatever growth you get from your investment in a TFSA is not subject to income tax. While most Canadians invest in a savings account, the account only fulfills its purpose when you earn a good return on your investment and do not pay tax on that return. The maximum amount you may contribute to a TFSA in 2022 is $6,000. If you have been in the country or are over eighteen years old and have not contributed in the past, you have a contribution room available for those years that can increase the limit that you can invest in a TFSA. If you are planning to buy a house, any money that is not contributed to an RRSP should be deposited into a tax-free savings account until the time of purchase. TFSA is a modern-day free gift from the Canadian government because of the zero tax on any gains or profit made in the account.

Michael had $20,000 in his savings account, earning 1% interest or $200 per year. He decided to transfer this amount to his TFSA, and he bought stocks of Pfizer and Netflix in March 2020. The pandemic had depressed the share value of both companies, but he felt that if people stayed at home, they would have to watch TV. And if any company were to find a cure for COVID-19, Pfizer would be one of them. So, he invested $10,000 in each stock. By December 2020, both stocks did well. The Netflix stock was worth $17,000, and the Pfizer stock was $13,000. So, he made a total of $10,000 profit. He did not owe any tax on the growth of his account because he made that money/gain in a TFSA.

Test Your Knowledge of This Chapter:

1. How do you lose money in a guaranteed investment?

2. What's the minimum return a mutual fund should be making every year over a period?

3. What kind of investment is good for business owners and why?

4. What's an ETF or Index Fund?

5. What's the easiest way to determine what stocks to invest in?

6. What is the job of a financial planner?

Chapter 12:

OTHER INVESTMENTS

There are so many different types of investments, and the details of how to use them is not within the scope of this book. We will however take a cursory look at a few that are available in Canada. You should not attempt to invest in any of them without first taking the time to learn more about them.

Trading in Options

An "option" gives you the right to buy an underlying security but not the obligation to do so. Options exist in the real estate industry, film, book industry, et cetera. In the securities market, options exist on most of the stocks available on the stock exchange. There are "call options" (the right to buy) and "put options" (the right to sell). These options usually expire on the third Friday of the month, and you can buy or sell an option for several months into the future. There are two parties to each transaction: the person who is writing the call and the buyer of the call or the person who is writing the put and the buyer of the put. Most people do not take delivery of call or put options, that is, they do not wait until expiry to settle the options they have bought or sold. Instead, they typically sell the options when it has appreciated or depreciated to the value they desire, thereby making a profit on fluctuating values of the product. Options are highly risky; you can literally lose all the invested money. It is important that you take an options course or lecture before you invest your hard-earned dollars in this volatile security.

A hypothetical example is Romeo who had no Juliet, but he had a TFSA (Tax free Savings Account) with a discount brokerage. He had $20,000 in it and decided to invest $5,000 in options and the rest in stocks. Romeo used $15,000 to buy stocks of banks and utility companies to get stable growth and dividends. He then bought a call option of Tesla in April 2021 (TSLA June 18, 2021, at $1,050, the price was $35.67). This meant that Romeo paid $35.67 per option (each option has 100 units) or $3,567. The Option expiry date was Jun 18th 2021 and he has the right to buy it for $1,050. At the time the price of one Tesla share was $610. When the price of the shares fluctuates, the price of the options fluctuates in great multiples of it. So by May of 2021, Tesla shares was trading for $1,050, the option traded for $121.34 or $12,134 which is a 340% increase. If in June of 2021 the Tesla stock had gone down in value to $490, the options would have been worth -$3,481 or a loss of -97.6%.

Short Selling

When you have an options account, you can short sell stocks, which means you can borrow securities that you don't own and sell them at the current market price, hoping to repurchase them in the future. This can be quite risky as the stock you sold can go up indefinitely from then on, and you may end up in debt. My advice is to take a course or lecture on these securities before investing in them, and if you do, let the amount invested be a small fraction of your portfolio.

John Smith short sells Tesla stocks in Apr of 2021 at $610, and he sells 100 shares. He immediately gets credited $61,000 in his brokerage account. If the price of Tesla stock goes down to $510, he will use the money in his account to buy back 100 shares for $51,000 and keep $10,000 as profit. If Tesla share continues to climb indefinitely, he is on the hook to buy back those shares at the price they become. The brokerage will, therefore, from time to time, make a margin call to him to keep a certain percentage of the value of the stock in his account.

Cryptocurrencies

Cryptocurrency is digital money that is used to do verified transactions in cryptography (writing and solving codes), but it does not have a controlling authority and the transaction records are maintained through a network of computers. They are not backed by anything, and their value stems from speculation. Transactions done in cryptocurrency are secure and visible, but you cannot tell who the purchaser or recipient is, hence the difficulty of being regulated by any government. To trade in this currency, you must buy it through an exchange like Coinbase or Binance. You purchase it using a credit card or PayPal, so they do not expose your credit information in places you don't want. Next, you need a digital wallet to store your currency. There are several of them, like Trust Wallet or Electroleum, where your money is digital, and you can trade with others using it easily. These are called hot wallets. With the other type of wallet, called a cold wallet, you need a device like a flash drive where you load the cryptocurrency. While the cold wallet is safer than the hot wallet, it is difficult to transfer to pay for goods and services. Many people use cryptocurrency for speculation. One bitcoin was equivalent to $20 in 2017; it grew to about $20,000 in 2020, in April of 2022 it grew to $57,317, and January of 2023 its back to $22,765. If you want to invest in cryptocurrency (crypto), you must do your research and be willing to lose whatever money you are investing in it. Bitcoin is the largest and most popular crypto and it is not yet legal tender in Canada and most countries. Still, because of its lax regulatory environment people with money from drug sales, proceeds of crime, and individuals and businesses that want to avoid anti-money-laundering regulations find cryptos very attractive. USDT is a crypto that is pegged to the US dollar so that people who want to make payments using cryptocurrency but don't want to speculate on the exchange rates can use it and it has become popular over the last few years.

> *Diego bought $8,000 worth of bitcoins in 2016 through a crypto broker and stored the money in a cold wallet for speculations and safety purposes. He kept the USB in his drawer. His little brother Miguel played with the USB when Diego was away in school and broke it. To hide what he did, Miguel threw it out. In 2020, bitcoin was trading at $20,000, and Diego decided it was time to cash out but could not find his USB. All that money was lost and can't be retrieved.*
>
> *In 2019, Gerald Cotton, the CEO of Quadriga, a cryptocurrency exchange, died while travelling. He had all the passwords of the exchange stored digitally. Being a thirty-year-old, he was not expected to die. Now, $145 million of bitcoin cannot be accessed by the company, so the owners are stuck.*
>
> *In Dec 2022 Samuel Bankman-Fried the CEO of FTX Cryptocurrency was arrested and charged with fraud. He had milked away client funds over the years and did it through multiple companies, deceiving a host of investors.*

Forex Trading

Forex trading is the act of buying and selling currencies. Every country has its own money (currency), and it has an exchange value for other countries' currencies. This exchange rate changes every second of the day and traders try to make a profit from buying or selling these currencies. They are usually bought and sold (traded) in pairs: USD/GBP means the US dollars versus the Great British pound, USD/CAD means the US dollars versus the Canadian dollar. All the major currencies are available on the money market to trade. Forex trading is legal in Canada, and it is regulated. Brokers like interactive brokers and CMC markets are available to the public. Most forex traders allow you to open a demo account, and they offer online classes to teach you how to trade in foreign currency. Once you learn the basics, you can use the demo account to test your knowledge and ability to pick the winning currencies before you start using real money to trade. All your transactions are online, so you can trade from anywhere in the world. You usually only have to deposit a very small percentage of the value of the position you hold. This is highly leveraged, which means your gains or losses will be highly magnified. Therefore, you need to do your research and know why you are trading what currency and be willing to see significant swings in amounts of money more considerable than what you have.

Sandra is British but lives in Canada. She likes the idea of trading in foreign currencies and has, for the last three years, been betting on the two currency pairs of Euro to US dollars and US dollars to Canadian dollars. She follows all the news and economic calendar in all regions and trades in small lot sizes every day. She started with $2,000 and has grown her investment to $6,200 in three years.

There are many trading styles and many strategies that can be employed; however, statistics show that 90% of retail traders lose 90% of their investments in one year or less. It is important that you take a course to learn about Forex Trading before you start. You should choose the strategy you will employ and stick to it while investing only amounts you are willing to lose.

Other Instruments

There are several other investment instruments available like Commodities, Metals and Minerals Trading, where you invest in the market by buying contracts on things like soybean, wheat, oil, cocoa, copper and gold. There is also the market for CFDs (Contracts for difference) sold heavily online by Forex and Commodities brokerages. These allow you to trade in futures. You buy a contract that predicts a future value, positive or negative. You are basically making a bet on the market's direction, and you only need a fraction of the amount you are trading in to start because the rest is leveraged. This is highly risky as the potential for growth and loss is very high if your prediction is right or wrong. These are not within the scope of this book, and I recommend you take a course to learn about them before you invest in such products. Other products include mezzanine financing, where you loan money to reputable builders who have land and a project they want to develop and need money to put the deal together and prepare till the bank finances their project. They usually pay a higher interest rate than the banks and offer their land as collateral. There are commercial papers, treasury bills, and many instruments that bankers or people with substantial money invest in. Some private lenders lend money to businesses and people who don't qualify for mortgages the traditional way. Whatever investment you choose, first do your research. Before investing, ask people in the industry, consult experts, and remember that investing should not be done with emotions. You need to research, analyze, and plan what you want to do and then do it. If you have a friend who might be interested in the same thing, engage them so that you can both learn together. Some TV stations focus on investing, like BNN, CNBC, Bloomberg, and others. If you watch such channels regularly, you will get to know what's going on in the investment world. Although it does not mean that you should follow recommendations you hear on them blindly, they typically have good analysts and insights that you might not have thought about.

Accredited investors: There are some investments that are only available to accredited investors and anyone selling you such an investment must ask you questions to make sure you qualify as one. If you meet any of the following criteria, you should qualify as one.

1. You earn over $200,000 annually, for at least two years.

2. Your total assets exceed $5,000,000.

3. Your investible assets are more than $1,000,000.

4. You are licensed as an adviser or dealer in Canada.

Test Your Knowledge of This Chapter:

1. What is driving the price of cryptocurrency?

2. Who should invest in Forex?

3. Who should invest in Commodities, Futures, and CFDs.

4. Who is an accredited investor?

Chapter 13:

BUSINESS OWNERSHIP

There are different types of businesses: sole proprietors, partnerships, limited liability corporations, and publicly traded companies. To register a business, you can either do it yourself, do it through many online services, or do it through a lawyer or an accountant. The process is straightforward, and depending on the route you take, it could cost you anywhere between $100 and $2,500.

Sole Proprietor

A sole proprietor is a business owned by one person, typically doing one thing. It may or may not be registered if the owner uses their name. Otherwise, they must register the name if they want to use a business name. The cost is minimal, from about $25 to $500, depending on who does the registration. You can open an account in your name or the business name and receive checks paid to either.

You and the business are one and the same for income tax purposes and liability issues.

> *Mr. Dwight Howard is a plumber and sole proprietor of his business. He registered as Howard Plumbing Enterprises. When opening a bank account, he will be able to receive checks in the name of Dwight Howard and Howard Plumbing Enterprises. He files his taxes as Dwight Howard, and there is no distinction between him and the enterprise he runs.*

Partnerships

With partnerships, you can also choose to register or not register a business name. This type of entity is good for professionals like lawyers, accountants, and others who work together. There are general partners and limited liability partners. As the name suggests, general partners are equally liable, while limited partners are only liable up to their ownership interest in the partnership. The business name registration is like that of the sole proprietors. For tax purposes, any income of the partnership is divided according to the partnership interest of each person and taxed in the hands of the individual partners.

Peter and Paul start a partnership to offer grass cutting services in the Greater Toronto Area. They have 70% and 30% ownership, respectively. So, when they are splitting the profit at year-end, Peter gets 70% of it, and Paul gets 30%. Their liability is also split the same way.

There is also a type of partnership called a limited liability partnership, where the liability of some of the partners is limited only to the amount they invested. So, take the case of Peter and Paul; if Peter was a general partner and Paul was a limited liability partner, then, if the business were to go bust, Paul only loses his 30% investment. In contrast, Peter would be personally liable for the entire liability of the entity because he is a general partner.

Corporation or Limited Liability Company

This type of business is a legal entity. It exists by itself and is a tax entity on its own and can sue or be sued. A corporation has its own tax bracket, pays its own taxes, and the corporation's liabilities are limited to the corporation. Most businesses function in this manner. Some people just register a numbered company if the business's name is not essential to the functions they want to use it for. A corporation can pay dividends or a share of its profits to its shareholders. This can lead to double taxation because you first pay taxes as a corporation, and then when you, the individual, receive dividends, you pay taxes again. Despite this disadvantage, a corporation is probably still the best way to do business because of the legal entity and liability issues. A corporation can make many deductions from its income before income tax is calculated and can exist forever.

A corporation can pay dividends to its shareholders, and you need a minimum of one shareholder to a maximum of fifty. All corporation names must end with Corporation, Corp, Limited, Ltd, Incorporated, or Inc.

> *Alex and Sheila decided to start a coffee shop in Hamilton; they wanted to run it as a corporation, so they registered/incorporated and called it Tasty Coffee Inc. They then invest money or get a loan under Tasty Coffee to run it. Tasty Coffee is, therefore, a separate entity from Alex and Sheila, and they become shareholders of the corporation. Tasty Coffee must have a financial year-end and file income taxes. Alex and Sheila can be employees of Tasty Coffee and get paid a salary and receive dividends as shareholders of Tasty Coffee.*

Publicly Traded Companies

These corporations have their shares traded on the stock exchange and must report their financial activities to the public and be accountable to their shareholders. They will typically have more than fifty shareholders and list with one or more stock exchanges. Most publicly traded companies start out as regular corporations until they grow big and need to raise funds from the public through an Initial Public Offering (IPO). To register a business, you can go to the Corporations Canada website to register a federal business or any of the provincial for-profit partners that do business registrations like incorporationpro.ca, corporationcenter.ca, ESC Corporate Services, and many others.

Suppose Tasty Coffee becomes highly successful in Hamilton, and Alex and Sheila want to expand it across Canada, and they don't have enough money for the expansion. They can decide to raise capital through the stock market. When they raise money in this manner from the public, they become a publicly-traded company and become accountable to their shareholders and their board of directors. This is how most giant corporations we know today started and grew till they became household names.

Starting Your Own Business

Being an entrepreneur is probably one of the best things you can be in Canada as 99.8% of businesses in Canada are small businesses or mid-sized businesses. A small business has one to hundred employees, and a mid-size has hundred to five hundred employees. They are scattered across all provinces and different sectors of the economy. You need to have the right mindset and discipline to be a small business owner.

Here are a couple of resources available to you:

- www.BDC.ca helps with loans, financing, and advisory services for businesses.
- The Big 6 banks also have business advisors or business development managers who handle financing for small businesses.

Your Business Plan

Before starting a business, you need a business plan. If correctly done, a business plan helps you write down your thoughts concerning all the different things you are supposed to consider before starting a business. It is a tool that will serve as a guide or road map to let you know what you want to do or accomplish, and it will also serve as a document that your financiers or potential investors can use to understand what you are doing. You can get free business plan templates on the BDC website and Google. If you struggle with the accounting/financing part of the business plan, you can pay a final-year accounting student some money to help with it.

Once you have put together a business plan, the next step is to do it. Depending on what you are doing and what you can afford, you might have to start with a home office or shared rental space. You might have to wear different hats based on your ability to hire staff. Whatever the case, just do what you have envisioned to do, and with diligence and time, you will become profitable.

Most structured institutions do not lend to new businesses, but they can give you a Home Equity Loan. There are, however, a large number of private equity and loans available in Canada, including mortgage lenders, commercial lenders, and other independent loan agencies. So, if your business requires funding, keep looking, and you will find the right solution for you. However, be very careful getting loans from predatory lenders or sharks who would tie your hands in such a manner that you can end up losing your home, business, or whatever collateral you have put down. Make sure to hire your own lawyer to review the documents you need to sign, so you don't lose your shirt. While the risks are high, owning a business gives the most reward. It rewards you financially and gives you the freedom to control your time and activity. Once it takes off, be sure to file your annual taxes, pay necessary bills, use insurance to protect yourself and your business, and remember to rest and take time off. In the pursuit of making more and more money, most small business owners have forgotten why they started the business in the first place. The challenges can be many. It might be difficult to find trustworthy staff, but your life can be heaven on earth once you do.

Neetu loves to bake and has always wanted to own a bakery. She did some research and found that there were no bakeries near a new condo development. Then she wrote a business plan, including:

- *What she would sell*
- *Staff requirements*
- *Her logo and potential marketing ideas*
- *Suppliers for her ingredients*
- *Her customer base*
- *Her experience and passion for the business as the director*
- *Information about her competitors, industry, and local area*
- *Financial Analysis and Growth Analysis*

After writing it, she approached Kelly, a final-year account-
ing student at the University of Toronto. She asked her to help
estimate her income and expense projections and forecast her
sales. Then, when the business plan was complete, she took it
to her bank to request a loan to pay for retrofitting a store she
wanted to lease. Seeing that she had signed and paid the lease
and had savings she would inject into the business for opera-
tions, the banker gave her a $60,000 loan for the renovation.
Neetu opened Neetu's Bake & Shake two months later and has
since become quite successful in the neighbourhood.

Buying a Business or Franchise

Whether buying a business or a franchise, you need to engage a good accountant, lawyer, commercial realtor, and commercial loan broker. Most of them have trusted people in their networks who offer these services.

Many immigrants opt to buy a business or a resale franchise, mainly because it is an immediate income-generating investment. You know the price going in, and you know the goodwill of previous clients in the location or the customers. Commercial real estate agents sell these. Also, there are various websites where you can find businesses for sale, like Realtor.ca, thebizex.com, Canadabusinessforsale. com, and many others. For most of them, you must take over the business and the existing lease, and some will allow you to change locations. You can get loans from lenders if you have a significant down payment and good credit.

Some businesses are just not being run well and need steady hands. Others have absentee owners and are not profitable. Still more are sold due to retirement or ailing health of the owner or owners moving out of the area or province. Whatever the reason, you must do your due diligence. The sellers will have you sign a non-disclosure agreement before sending you the details about the business. Make sure the numbers work for you. It must be the type of business you see yourself doing long-term and can commit to building.

If you are patient enough, you can also buy franchises directly from the company that owns the business called the franchisor. For example, Dave Thomas of the Wendy's Burger Chain franchise, owned three KFC franchises before starting Wendy's. If managed well and the location is good, these can be very profitable. Once you own one franchise and run it well, adding two or three more is easy as you already know how it works. Apart from owning the business, each franchise owner can earn a handsome salary.

I had a husband-and-wife clients who were project managers. They bought a Tim Hortons' franchise. At the time, it cost only $250,000. The husband resigned and ran it when they started while the wife brought home the steady income. Within weeks of opening, he was able to draw a $70,000 annual salary from the business. They grew and later employed the wife as manager. Within two years, they opened two other Tim Hortons' franchises and paid themselves the same salary at each one.

Test Your Knowledge of This Chapter:

1. What is a corporation?

2. How do you write a business plan?

3. What kind of business can you do if you have no business idea of your own?

Chapter 14:

RISK TOLERANCE

In the foreword to this book, we discussed risks and rewards. Now that we have reviewed most of the different types of investments in the marketplace, it is prudent that we dedicate this chapter to discussing risks from the angle of fear or possibility of loss. This is probably the most important of all the chapters. Risk in the marketplace is exposure to a possibility of loss, and it exists in every investment you make except for Treasury Bills and Guaranteed Investment Certificates (GICs). You, therefore, must know how comfortable you are with the risk involved in any investment before you invest.

When there is an offer to pursue an investment, most people think primarily about the returns on the investment. They are excited about it, or when listening to a knowledgeable advisor or friend who has made money doing it, they feel exhilarated and jump into the investment based on emotions. Others hear of the investment and examine the risk and the fear of loss keeps them from taking the step they know they should take. As humans, we have various levels of risk tolerance. Some people can bungee jump, and some can skydive, while others are not even comfortable flying in an airplane. I remember visiting an amusement park, and you could hear people screaming out of excitement in the distance. Others were moaning or walking around sadly because they could not get on any rides. When forced or tricked into going on some rides, some will go and end up crying, peeing in their pants, or doing something totally strange. I have even seen someone screaming on a carousel, which most consider one of the safest rides in a park. This shows that our risk levels are as unique to us as our DNA. So it is with investments, we have unique risk levels that can be similar to or very different from others. Therefore, whatever thing you decide to do, you must determine the risk involved and know if you are comfortable with it. Some risks are obvious and some are not. Some risks can be mitigated, others cannot. You can reduce some risks by doing something different with your other assets, and some are just not worth taking the risk. At times, the fear of loss is just based on the lack of knowledge in an area and not so much on the fact that the investment is a high-risk product. After you educate yourself about the investment, you can move up on the risk spectrum of that product. Let us examine some risks in some of the products you have read about and tactics to mitigate them.

Mutual funds, for example, are a basket or combination of several different securities, apart from the money market fund that is full of treasury bills and the like. All mutual funds fluctuate in value, but because it is a basket, the fund managers include several different stocks or bonds in various combinations depending on the type of fund. If a few go down in value, others will go up in value. In that sense, they have reduced the overall risk of having just one security. If you had a fund that holds fifty to hundred stocks, technically speaking, all hundred companies can go bankrupt. Their shares become worthless; in which case, you lose all your money. Still, it is not probable as some companies are household names and part and parcel of our everyday lives. Global conglomerates are doing business in different regions, and some businesses produce goods and services that the government and society benefit from, so it is not likely to happen. If you had a growth Mutual fund with 80% of its investments in stocks and 20% in bonds, the 20% bonds are investments in government and provincial government instruments which is backed by the strength of those economies. Suppose, 80% is invested in companies like the six major banks in Canada: RBC, TD, CIBC, BMO, BNS, and National Bank. Or it might be in the companies that supplies gas to our homes and cars like Enbridge and Suncor. It could be those department stores and grocers like Loblaws and Walmart, our insurance companies like Sunlife and Manulife, and our cable and telephone companies like Rogers and Bell. I think you get my drift, and you can see that it is not probable that you can lose your money when you invest in these over a long period of time. Things can happen in the short term that can make portfolios dip, but they usually will come back in value if you stay invested.

> *At the beginning of the COVID-19 pandemic, I had just invested in my RRSP in February 2020 and noted the balance (I don't look at the balance of my long-term account regularly as it can tempt you to make short-term decisions). By the end of March, my portfolio had dropped by 20%. It fluctuated for about five months and began to climb. By December, it had gone up 25% from its March value. I would have lost money if I had sold when it was down. Now that it is up, I still will not sell because the money is for my retirement, which is more than ten years away.*

Segregated funds and ETFs follow this same risk rule as mutual funds. As for Bonds, the issuer guarantees the bond, however, your bond interest rate and the interest rate that prevails in the markets at different times can cause your bonds to go up and down in value. In addition, if you hold on to your bond until maturity, you will get the full interest promised and your money back. But it is possible that the bond's issuer goes bankrupt and cannot pay you your money or the interest promised. It can happen in some cases; it is not probable in others. The kind of bonds where the issuer's stability is in question are called junk bonds. They pay a higher interest rate and are highly risky. As for the investment-grade bonds, the rating agencies' job is to review each issuer's financials and give it a grade or rating. So, the Canadian government bond is AAA, and the US is AA, while the Mexican government is BBB. It's based on their ability to repay, and because countries have people to tax and companies have people buying their products, it is not probable.

In the early 2000s, World Com and Enron falsified their books and deceived even the best of analysts. When their lie became public, the stocks crashed to pennies, and creditors seized their assets. Bondholders came second place to creditors. The US government created the Sarbanes Oxley Act (SOX), which now dictates how public companies must be governed for investor protection. In Canada we have the Canadian SOX (C-SOX) which does the same thing.

With insurance, it is interesting because, with anything you do not insure, you are the one bearing the risk. For example, if you do not have Critical Illness Insurance, you bear the risk where you suffer the financial consequence if you fall critically ill. On the other hand, if you insure and the event occurs, what happens if the company does not or cannot pay? In Canada, about ten big insurance companies do all kinds of insurance, and they also sell those insurance products to reassurance companies. Once the risk covered in the policy document is clear and there is no foul play, they typically will pay and can afford to. In the US, during the Subprime lending crisis, an insurance company called AIG had made a bad investment in debt instruments linked to the crises; they were too big to fail. The government came to their aid. They ended up selling their operations worldwide to different companies to not collapse the market and erode confidence in the market. They were a threat to the US market. BMO bought their Canadian arm in 2009. As of 2020, AIG was no longer a threat to the US market and is once again functioning and doing business worldwide, including in Canada.

Some people believe that because a real estate investment is brick and mortar and you can see it physically, there is no risk; this is far from the truth. The reason you make money in real estate is because of leverage. I have been investing in real estate since 2003, and while I have made money, I have had my share of issues. What if you buy the house, get a mortgage, and the housing market crashes, and your home is worth less than the value you paid for it? Well, because the alternative is that you rent and 100% of your rent is gone forever, this argument is lame because if you continue to make your mortgage payments, you will one day be mortgage-free and own the house, whatever the value is at that time. What if it's time to renew your mortgage and interest rates are so high that you cannot afford the payment? Most people buying a home for the first time usually lock in the rates for five years so at least they know the fixed amount they will pay for five years. If your situation deteriorates in five years instead of improving or the country's interest rate goes through the roof, you can at least sell and cash in the equity you have built up.

As for rental properties, what if you buy them and no one wants to rent them? What if a tenant rents it and does not make the payment, and now you are stuck with paying your own mortgage and that of the rental? I have been in both situations. The first rental we bought took over two months to renovate and find a tenant. The realtor we had was not very knowledgeable about rental properties and why this particular house was not a good investment. It was a bungalow in Scarborough with a basement apartment; it was not close to the main road or subway. I was a newbie and had no relationships with contractors and handymen; it needed a lot of renovation. Most people who stayed in basement apartments at the time did not have cars. When we finally rented out both apartments, I got calls from one tenant complaining about the other tenant. It was so bad that we sold the house within one year. Though the house sold for slightly higher than the price we paid, our calculation shows we had an overall loss. Because all the money that went into renovating the house was not recovered. Also, we had wasted a lot of time on it. This experience made us change the way we viewed real estate and from then on, we planned and made our own decisions and executed without external directions.

We decided to buy new homes as they would not need renovation. They would appeal to tenants. We could rent single units to families in slightly better neighbourhoods with people of somewhat better income. So, we bought one, rented it out in less than one week, bought the next one, rented it out in less than a month, and that is how we started our portfolio of investment in real estate.

Buying or starting a business or franchise is risky. Even though you made good plans and did all the right stuff, it does not mean that it is an automatic success. If it were that easy, then everyone would do it. Still, because not everyone is willing to take up the challenge, those who take up the challenge and find different ways of dealing with the obstacles they face, eventually get rewarded with success.

Cryptocurrencies are a relatively new area in the world of finance. The currencies have not become legal tender, but they are not illegal, so the risk is that we can wake up one day, and the government will declare them illegal and shut them down. This is possible but not probable as different large retailers and companies now allow purchases using the currency online. The cryptocurrency you buy can go bust. There is a lot of misinformation about them and forward-looking statements online. We expect this because everyone is speculating. My recommendation is not to invest more than you are willing to lose.

Forex, commodity trading, options trading, and any type of investment involving derivatives and leverage are highly risky. So, the first step in these types of investments is to attend a course or training about them. The second is to make sure you have a stop-loss order that limits your downside risk to what you can afford to lose.

Even in playing the lottery, you can end up investing $20,000 or more over your lifetime in something you get a zero return on, and all the principal is lost.

Whatever you do, you can always find a reason not to invest, and you can always find a risk that you cannot reduce or avoid. If you cannot afford to do it now, maybe you can in the future, but remember that investments are not to be made based on emotions because your emotions will deceive you. I am yet to find one person who bought a home and did not go home and think, "Did I make the right decision? Should I have signed for such a large mortgage, or what if this or that?" It is called buyer's remorse. In the securities market, people are happy when they are up in value and sad when they are down.

In 2001, I was trading in options on Nortel Networks. I was new in the investment industry, and I did not have a lot of money, so I borrowed $10,000 from my line of credit and started to trade. Every day, the portfolio would go up 30%, then drop 50%. It was so volatile that I began to dream about it. I could not sleep; I just kept seeing up and down in my sleep, my blood pressure was up, and I eventually sold at $4,000 because I realized that no investment was worth the health risk I was facing. It made me stop investing in options till nineteen years later. This time, I was in a better financial position. I had not borrowed the money at risk, the fluctuations did not bother me, and I had put stop losses on them to limit my risk. So, the investment that is not right for you in one season of your life might be okay in another season. My personality type is such that I am a runner. Once I find out about something, while others are still thinking about it, I review and try it out. So, for those who are like me pause and do your research, weigh the risk, and plan before you execute.

Test Your Knowledge of This Chapter:

1. What does it mean if you buy an investment and you can't sleep?

2. When is there no fear of loss in an investment that is not guaranteed?

3. What does it mean if an investment loss is possible but not probable?

4. What can you do if you think an investment is risky but it's mainly because you don't know about it?

Chapter 15:

FAITH

I am writing this chapter for people of the Christian faith. If that does not apply to you, you can skip to the concluding chapter now, and you will still get the full value of the book.

Many Christians do not understand the Bible and the world of finance, and many church leaders do not either. I have listened to many sermons where the preachers tell their congregations to give, and God will bless them. Yet, I have watched hundreds give and believe, year in and year out, and they are still in the same situation. They become dejected, and at some point, they cease believing in God for a financial breakthrough. So, let's examine what God thinks of his children prospering.

First, we start with a few scriptures:

Let the Lord be magnified, which takes pleasure in the prosperity of his servant. (Psalms 35:27)

And God blessed them, and God said unto them, be fruitful, and multiply, and replenish the earth, and subdue it and have dominion over the fish of the sea and the fowl of the air and over every living thing that moves upon the earth. (Genesis 1:28)

And God blessed Noah and his sons and said unto them be fruitful and multiply and replenish the earth. (Genesis 9:1)

While the earth remains, seedtime and harvest, and cold and heat, and summer and winter, and day and night shall not cease. (Genesis 8:22)

These verses list a host of blessings that God desires his people to have. (Deuteronomy 28:1–14)

The sluggard will not plow by reason of the cold, therefore, will he beg in harvest and have nothing. (Proverbs 20:4)

Bring ye all the tithe into my storehouse and prove me, if I will not open the windows of heaven and pour you out a blessing that there shall not be room enough to receive it and I will rebuke the devourer for your sakes. (Malachi 3:10)

The first thing we must understand is that it was mainly an agrarian society in the Bible days, which means agriculture was what most people were involved in. So, everyone could understand the concepts used from that point of view. Today, we are industrialized, we have technology, and information is easily accessible from everywhere. So, the principles of the lessons remain the same, but the content is different. For example, with seedtime and harvest, sowing seeds and reaping is used to teach giving principles that when you give money or anything, it is multiplied back to you in return. This principle is true, but I want us to take a different look at some of the principles taught in the Bible and apply them in the world of finance.

In Luke 19:1–27, a man named Zacchaeus was a senior tax collector (senior CRA tax advisor). The Jewish people (church people) hated the tax advisors because the tax collection system in those days was arbitrary. The collector levied you an amount. He took the money from you, kept back part of it, and gave the remaining to the government (the tax collectors were wealthy, although mostly fraudulent). Zacchaeus wanted to see Jesus, so he climbed up a tree for he was short, and when Jesus got to the tree, he asked him to come down as he would have lunch with him at his house, which made Zacchaeus happy and all the church people mad and sad. Zacchaeus then said he would give half of his wealth to charity, and to anyone he had taken money from by false accusation, he will give him back four times as much of his money; this is 400% profit on the refund. Jesus exclaimed that Salvation had come to Zacchaeus's household as he was also a son of Abraham (a child of God) because Jesus came to save everyone who was lost. Jesus then tells this parable.

Luke 19:12–27

King James Version

^{12} *He said therefore, "A certain nobleman went into a far country to receive for himself a kingdom, and to return."*

^{13} *And he called his ten servants, and delivered them ten pounds, and said unto them, "Occupy till I come."*

^{14} *But his citizens hated him and sent a message after him, saying, "We will not have this man to reign over us."*

^{15} *And it came to pass that when he was returned, having received the kingdom, then he commanded these servants to be called unto him,* to whom he had given the money, that he might know how much every man had gained by trading.

¹⁶ Then came the first, saying, "Lord, thy pound hath gained ten pounds."

¹⁷ And he said unto him, "Well, thou good servant: because thou hast been faithful in a very little, have thou authority over ten cities."

¹⁸ And the second came, saying, "Lord, thy pound hath gained five pounds."

¹⁹ And he said likewise to him, "Be thou also over five cities."

²⁰ And another came, saying, "Lord, behold, here is thy pound, which I have kept laid up in a napkin:

²¹ For I feared thee, because thou art an austere man: thou takest up that thou layedst not down, and reapest that thou didst not sow."

²² And he saith unto him, "Out of thine own mouth will I judge thee, thou wicked servant. Thou knewest that I was an austere man, taking up that I laid not down, and reaping that I did not sow:

²³ Wherefore then gavest not thou my money into the bank, that at my coming I might have required mine own with usury?"

²⁴ And he said unto them that stood by, "Take from him the pound, and give it to him that hath ten pounds."

²⁵ (And they said unto him, Lord, he hath ten pounds.)

²⁶ For I say unto you, "That unto every one which hath shall be given; and from him that hath not, even that he hath shall be taken away from him."

²⁷ But those mine enemies, which would not that I should reign over them, bring hither, and slay them before me.

The noble man is Jesus, who has gone away and left his servants, who are believers, with some money with instructions to occupy till he comes back. Many people of the world did not like him, and obviously, they would have made sure it was not easy for his believers to occupy till the master returned. And after a long time, the master returned and asked his people to give an account of the monies he had given them.

The first servant traded with the money he had received. In today's world, we use the word trading in doing business, buying and selling stocks, buying and selling foreign exchange, and buying and selling commodities. Other things people trade in today include art collections, real estate, and rare products like vintage cars, rare coins, and even running shoes.

His one pound had gained ten pounds or a 1,000% profit, and his master made him ruler over ten cities. The other servant's one pound had gained five pounds or 500% profit. The trading activities listed above are the only types of activities in our current world where you can get those types of returns. With businesses, most that make these kinds of profits get to operate in multiple cities or nations.

For example, when Walmart listed its shares on the stock exchange on October 1, 1970, it sold each share for $16.50 and had 300,000 shares. If an investor bought a hundred of those shares at that time for $1,650, it is now valued at $4.3 million; this is well over 2,500%. When Microsoft was listed on March 13, 1986, each share sold for $21. Microsoft shares have split nine times, so $100 would have gotten four shares, and today would be 28,000 shares. Microsoft trades at $212 now; the value is $5,936,000 which is a 59,360% return. Therefore, they get to trade in all the countries of the world if they multiplied what the master gave them. If you notice, not only has Microsoft or Bill Gates done well, but those who invested in the corporation's stock have done well too.

The servant who got the one pound said he was afraid of losing the master's money, so rather than placing it in a GIC or savings account at the bank, he decided to hide it in his safe or under his mattress. The master told him that the least he could have done was to put it in a savings account for a paltry interest, and then he took it from him and gave it to the servant who knew what to do with it. When I worked at the bank, we had countless customers who kept $40,000, $120,000, and $380,000 in savings accounts, earning 0.002% for months. It was my job to call up these clients to show them a better way.

Aby was fifty-eight when I met her in 2007. She had one daughter, a home, and a dog. She was a corporate executive for years and was worried about retirement. Aby had about $520,000 in cash between her checking and savings account, which she had slowly saved up over twenty years. She did not trust any advisor as she had lost money earlier and swore not to invest again. After doing a thorough financial plan for her, she was at ease with me, and I moved her cash from checking and savings accounts into some balanced mutual funds and a bit into a dividend growth fund. By 2015, this minor change had resulted in her portfolio growth to $700,000, and she was able to retire comfortably. I always wondered what her portfolio would have looked like if I had met her earlier.

When you have money, it should be working for you daily. Bankers and investors know this principle. That is why the banks use deposits you give them, to loan money to other clients at a rate higher than what they are paying depositors. Cash is indeed king, but it's only king when it does something. It's not king when it's piled up doing nothing. There is a character in the Bible referred to by Jesus as the rich fool. Although he did not deserve to be mentioned by name, his agricultural business prospered very well. He decided to stop increasing his productivity, build a large storage chamber, store the increase, and live off his profits forever. Yet, after storing everything up, he died. We are to remain eternally productive and continue to use our assets and abilities to gain more and more till our time on earth expires.

In taking away the pound from him and giving it to the servant who got 1,000%, Jesus said, "To him that has more, more will be given and to him that has not, even that which he has shall be taken away," which confirms the saying that the "rich get richer, and the poor get poorer."

However, we can see that the poor are not destined for poverty, but the choices made by everyone over some time determine our future financial state. Some worked and invested hard when things were harsh, or when it was snowing, or when the market crashed, and it looked like they would lose everything. As a result, they went through emotional turmoil, yet ended up in a great place. Others played it safe; they earned a paycheck, paid their rent, did not care when the market crashed because they were not invested in the markets, and did not care when the housing market slumped because they did not own real estate. Eventually, they retired, got a government pension, and the money was barely enough to pay rent, so they moved in with their kids and became a burden on the new family, who also didn't have enough for rent. Hence, they split the rent, and the cycle continues.

In Acts 4:36, Joses Barnabas was called the son of consolation because he sold his real estate and used the money to benefit God's kingdom. It was his example that other believers were following, which in Acts 5 made Ananias and Sapphira sell their property and lie about how much they sold it for. Then, when they brought it to Peter, they wanted to get the glory of saying that they sold their land and brought all the money.

The church needs money to expand God's kingdom and benefit humanity. For example, Bill Gates could use his money to eradicate polio in the world. Countless rich people pay for university education for people who cannot afford it. Others provide food, support homeless shelters, and the list goes on. You must decide which side you want to be on. The one which is helping others or the one which needs help. If someone is helping you now, then decide to make choices that will lead you to a time when you will be the one doing the helping. It may seem dark now, but joy and light come in the morning. You have not been condemned to a state of poverty. God can and will get you out; you only have to believe and then put action to what you believe.

A feast is made for laughter and wine maketh merry: but money answers all things. (Ecclesiastes 10:19)

I have worked in investment companies, banks, and the church, and I have found that all organizations need money to function. The difference between a for-profit corporation and a charity is that the for-profit entity depends solely on its ingenuity and work to produce profits for its owners. In contrast, the church primarily depends on the goodwill of its donors to get the income it needs to do the work it desires to do. The church's charitable status does not permit it to do business. The idea would be great if they taught all members lessons that helped them become who God has destined them to be. Suppose they build businesses and educate themselves enough to earn high incomes and function at the highest level, and they, in turn, consistently give a portion of their income to the church. In that case, the church will have enough income to do all the charitable work they desire to do. Unfortunately, in this age where churches are set up without proper structures and run in a mum and pop fashion, many believers are told to give, and God will bless them. However, they often ignore the other visioning principles, developing a relationship with the Holy Spirit, finding God's will for your life, engaging in business, studying, and developing a skill set. As a result, many churchgoers get disillusioned as they have been giving to God for decades, and nothing has changed, so they stop giving or just continue to wait. Everyone prosperous in the Bible did something. Abraham dug wells, and Isaac planted crops during the time of famine. Jacob was a cattle farmer who practiced crossbreeding, and though he lived off commission, God prospered him exceedingly. David's gift was a heart for God, and he was a worshiper. This got him before the king. He was a shepherd and a fighter who had the skill of shooting the sling. God used this skill to kill Goliath. Joseph was a dreamer who had a relationship with God and was skilled in management. God used his gift to bring him before the king and used the skill to manage the resources of the then known world. Even Solomon, the son of a rich king, ascended the throne and gave 1,000 burnt offerings to

God when he was asked. He prayed for wisdom and understanding. You can find his import and export business in 2 Chronicles 1:16–17 and his investments in Song of Songs 8:11–12; he leased out real estate to get 1,000, and the managers got 200. This means he got 83.33% of the profit, and the managers got 16.66%.

If you do not believe in tithes and offerings, just know that all the money you get in life is a seed, and you ought to give out of your seeds to something that does not benefit you directly so that, in the future, you will continue to have more seeds. But like any farmer, you do not plant seeds and then fold your hands to do nothing. You must go out every day to water the seed, keep the plant from weeds, and be present to pluck up the plants during harvest. This process is both spiritual and physical. The work you do, the business you do, and the investment you engage in are the places where you reap the seeds you have sown.

There are many scriptures we quote in the bible that do not apply to everyone. Philippians 4:19 says, *My God shall supply all your need according to his riches in glory through Christ*. If you read that scripture in context, Paul spoke to those who had enquired from him about giving and receiving and who had given to support the work of the ministry.

2 Corinthians 8 and 9 are must-reads for every believer to understand how to give and what to give. Do not be cajoled into giving what you do not plan to give or think that you are doing God a favour. God wants us to be happy and joyful and give to him out of a heart of gratitude and love as worship to him. Then, God pours out a blessing when all the taps are open. The number one area that brings an increase to anyone is giving to the poor. Psalms 112 shows

us how the man who has wealth and riches in God's eyes gets it, and we know that in Jesus's time, he gave to the poor (John 13:29). Job 29 reveals the secret of Job's success.

Test Your Knowledge of This Chapter:

1. Who are the people that are allowed to operate in different cities and countries?

2. What happens to people who are afraid to invest?

3. Mention some of the ways Bible characters earned money?

4. How do New Testament believers give?

Chapter 16:

CONCLUSION

Now that you have seen what the Canadian investment landscape holds, it's time for you to start making decisions about what you want in Canada, what you want out of life here, what things you will engage in, and what pitfalls you are going to avoid. Remember, if you fail to plan, you plan to fail. If you don't know where you are going, every road will lead you there. Take some time to reflect on what you have learned and how you would apply it to your life. Consider which investments you want to engage in and how you will do so. If someone recommends a product to you, consult this book before deciding.

If there are areas where you need more information, you can browse some of the websites provided at the end of this book. In addition, many people offer seminars and one-day courses on several topics. If you are going to be investing your hard-earned dollars, you might as well pay some money to someone to get you up to speed. There is no shame in asking questions, and no knowledge is ever wasted.

Because you have started your journey with this book, I know you are on track for success. The last thing for you to do is to engage the law of attraction, focus your mind on what you want, ask for it, believe you have it, and be thankful ahead of time. Then, you will have what you desire.

Please fill out the following questionnaire to tell your future self what you decided when you read this book.

RESOURCES

My Canadian Dream

On this date _____ 20_____, I, _____,
am grateful for being in Canada and I am thankful for all the
opportunities I have been afforded as a resident of this great country.
I want to learn more about the governing system of this nation and
all the financial and investment systems available to me.

My Vision:

I desire that I will:

_____

_____

_____

_____

Goals:

1._____

2._____

3._____

4._____

5._____

Investments:

I will own:

_____

_____

_____

_____

Time:

I will accomplish this by

_____

_____

_____

_____

WEBSITES

There are several websites that you can use to gain knowledge. Some have a subscription fee attached to giving investment suggestions, and some are very helpful when doing research.

1. General Knowledge: www.investopedia.com

2. Mutual Funds: www.mackenzieInvestmenst.com https://www.fidelity.ca/en/

3. Segregated Funds (Seg funds): www.equitable.ca, www.sunlife.ca

4. The Index or Indices: www.tsx.com, www.nasdaq.com

5. Exchange Traded Funds (ETF): www.bmoetf.ca, www.vanguardcanada.ca

6. Stocks (Shares): www.ca.finance, www.yahoo.com , www.fool.ca

7. Initial Public Offerings (IPOs): www.nasdaq.com www.marketwatch.com

8. Bonds: www.bloomberg.com

9. Investment Trusts: www.riocan.com , www.chartwell.com

10. Brokerage: www.edwardjones.ca , www.woodgundy.cibc.com

11. Discount Brokerage: www.tdwaterhouse.ca , www.quest-trade.ca

12. Financial Planning: www.bmo.com , www.investors-group.com

13. Insurance Advisor: http://www.ibc.ca/on/ (Check out each provincial regulator)

14. Trading in Options: www.tdwaterhouse.ca , www.bmoin-vestorline.ca

15. Credit: www.scotiabank.com , www.rbcroyalbank.com , www.cibc.com

16. Credit Bureau: www.consumer.equifax.ca , www.transunion.ca

17. Credit Products: www.td.com , www.bmo.com www.simpli.com

18. Pre-paid Credit Card: www.visa.ca , www.mastercard.ca, www.capitalone.ca

19. Department or Store Credit Card: www.homedepot.ca , www.thebrick.com

20. Student Credit Card: www.bmo.com , www.cibc.com www.td.com

21. Consumer Proposals/Bankruptcies: www.davidsklar.com , www.afarber.com

22. Loyalty Program: www.airmiles.ca , www.prioritypass.com

23. Buying a Home: www.realtor.ca , www.point2homes.com

24. Tax-Free Savings Account (TFSA): www.td.com , www.rbcroyalbank.com

25. Registered Plans: www.investorsgroup.com

26. Annuity: www.manulife.ca , www.freedon55financial.com

27. Employer Pension Plan: www.sunlife.ca

28. Life Insurance: www.canadalife.com www.equitablelife.ca, www.manulife.ca

29. Canada Pension Plan and OAS: www.canada.ca/en/ revenue-agency

30. Buying or Leasing Your First Car: www.autotrader.ca , www.carpages.ca

31. Breaking a Lease or Finance: www.leasebusters.com

32. Taxes: www.canada.ca/en/revenue-agency

33. Wills and Powers of Attorney: www.legalwills.ca

34. Buying Commercial Real Estate: www.realtor.ca , www.crea.ca

35. Business: www.bdc.ca , www.edc.ca

36. Business Registration: https://ised-isde.canada.ca/site/ised/en

37. Buying a Business: www.businessforsale.ca , www.bizex.com

38. Franchise: www.franchisegator.com , www.franchisedirectcanada.com

39. Charities: https://apps.cra-arc.gc.ca/ebci/hacc/srch/pub/ dsplyBscSrch?request_locale=en

40. Lottery: https://www.olg.ca/en/home.html

41. Currency trading: www.forex.com

42. Cryptocurrencies: www.coindesk.com , www.coinsmart.ca

43. Commodities: www.interactivebrokers.ca

References

1. https://www.investopedia.com/
   financial-term-dictionary-4769738

2. https://www.canada.ca/en/services/taxes/savings-and-
   pension-plans.html

3. Page 75/76 https://www.moneysense.ca/save/retirement/
   pensions/update-on-employer-pensions-and-more-in-
   the-november-issue-of-moneysense/

4. Page 171/172 https://www.biblegateway.com/
   passage/?search=Luke+19%3A12-27&version=KJV

5. Page 8 https://www.justice.gc.ca/eng/csj-sjc/rfc-dlc/ccrf-
   ccdl/rfcp-cdlp.html

6. Page 8 https://reviewlution.ca/resources/how-ma-
   ny-millionaires-in-canada/#:~:text=There%20are%20
   1%2C681%2C969%20Canadians%20with,or%20a%20
   million%20Canadian%20dollars.

7. Page 9 https://worldpopulationreview.com/countries

8. Page 9 https://www.cnbc.com/2021/12/22/her-
   es-how-22-million-americans-became-millionaires.html

GLOSSARY OF TERMS

Credit

Amortization: Length of time it will take to pay off a mortgage.

Bank of Canada: This is the central bank or arm of the government that regulates the monetary operations of the country.

Bank Rate: This is the rate the central bank lends to the banks.

Bankruptcy: When someone legally declares that they can no longer pay their debts and wants the creditors to discharge their obligations to pay it.

CMHC (Canada Mortgage and Housing Corporation): An agency of the government that insures mortgages for people who take out mortgages with the banks that is more than 80% of the value of the home.

Credit Bureau: The agency where all credit transactions are recorded, and lenders can check prospective borrower's credit history.

Credit History: The history of credit used, obtained from the Credit Bureau.

Credit Score: A number or score assigned to each individual that rates them as a credit user.

Emergency Funds: Money set or saved aside for emergencies, usually three to six months' expense amount.

Fixed Mortgage: A mortgage that has a fixed rate for a specific period.

Line of Credit: A revolving amount of credit that you can use repeatedly up to the approved limit.

Mortgage: A loan secured against real estate.

Mortgage Term: The time or period for which a mortgage rate is set.

Overdraft: A credit facility that allows you to draw more than the amount you have in your bank account.

Prime Rate: This is the lending rate the banks lend to their best customers.

Secured Line of Credit: A line of credit that is secured with an asset.

Students Line of Credit: A revolving credit given to students to pay for college or university education.

Variable Mortgage: A mortgage with rates that fluctuate during the specified term. It's usually linked to the prime lending rate.

Buying Your First Car

Car Lease: When you get a car to use for a certain period, pay a certain amount, and have a certain amount of milage to use.

Buying a Home

HBP (Home Buyers' Plan): A plan that allows you to borrow money from your RRSP to purchase your first home.

Saving for University or College

CESG (Canada Education Savings Grant): The grant the government contributes to each beneficiary's RESP plan.

CLB (Canada Learning Bond): The additional grant that is contributed to RESP plans for beneficiaries of a low-income family.

LLLP (Life-Long Learning Plan): A government plan that allows you to borrow money from your RRSP to finance higher education for yourself.

RESP (Registered Education Savings Plan): A government plan that helps you save for higher education for your children.

Retirement

Annuity: An insurance plan which you purchase with an amount of money and receive regular payments in return for life or for a fixed period.

CPP (Canada Pension Plan): This is the government pension plan for every worker who pays taxes and contributes during their years of employment.

DBP (Defined Benefit Pension): The original type of employer pension where the amount you receive is defined, adjusted to inflation, and last till death.

DCP (Defined Contribution Pension): The new type of employer pension where, you contribute a percentage of your income and the employer contributes a percentage of your income to a fund of your choice with the plan administrator appointed by your employer. At retirement, you draw from whatever amount is in the plan.

Employee Savings Plan (ESP) and Stock Options: A plan where your employer gives you a share of the company as incentive or bonus for your work.

HBP (Home Buyers' Plan): A plan that allows you to borrow money from your RRSP to purchase your first home.

Locked-in Retirement Income Fund (LRIF): This is a deaccumulation fund that transfers balances from the LRSP when you are retired and ready to start withdrawing money.

Locked-in Retirement Savings Plan (LRSP): This is a plan that allows people who have left their employment and have an employer pension plan to transfer that pension plan into it and the owner chooses the type of investment in it.

OAS (Old Age Security) and GIS (Guaranteed Income Supplement): These are plans put in place by the government to provide income to seniors.

RDSP (Registered Disability Savings Plan): A plan that allows you to save for a disabled child with tax benefits and grants.

RRIF (Registered Retirement Income Fund): A deaccumulation plan that is established to receive money accumulated from an RRSP in a tax advantaged manner.

RRSP (Registered Retirement Savings Plan): A plan established to save for retirement that gives a tax benefit to the owner.

Taxes and Charitable Giving

CRA (Canada Revenue Agency) This is the arm of the government that is responsible for taxes.

Donation Receipt: This is a tax receipt that you get when you give money to a charity. You can file this receipt with your annual return to save on taxes.

EI (Employment Insurance): An amount that each employee contributes to a government plan, that is matched by their employer. This plan provides benefits (income) to employees for a period of time if they stop work for specific reasons.

Income Tax: The tax that employers are required to take from an employee's salary and give to the government.

Goods and Service Tax (GST) and Harmonized Sales Tax (HST): These are taxes collected on the sales of goods and services on behalf of the government (CRA).

Income Tax Filing/Annual Return Filing: This is the process where you file to declare your income tax to the CRA, the government agency responsible for taxes.

Tax Avoidance: Using the tax laws to your benefit to pay less taxes.

Tax Evasion: Doing things illegally to not pay tax.

Insurance

Term Insurance: Life Insurance for a period of time, usually twenty to thirty years.

Whole Life: Insurance that covers you till death.

Wills and Powers of Attorney

Beneficiaries: The person or people who get the benefits of the will.

Executor: The person who does the administrative duties of settling the will.

Intestate: When someone dies without a will.

POA (Power of Attorney): A legal document that gives someone authority to act on behalf of another.

Testator: The person who is the owner of the will.

Will: Your last wishes or testament.

Death and the Lottery

Survivors Pension Benefit: Money paid by the government to the family of the deceased.

Real Estate Investing

Commercial Real Estate: These are properties that are primarily for business.

Principal Residence: The place where you live from a tax perspective. It could be your home or your cottage.

Residential Real Estate: These are properties that are primarily for people to live in.

The Investment Landscape

CDIC (Canada Deposit Insurance Corporation): An Agency of the government that protects the deposits at financial institutions that are members.

GIC (Guaranteed Investment Certificate): An investment issued by trust companies that offer a full guaranty of principal and interest up to a specified amount and is backed up by protection from CDIC a government agency.

IPO (Initial Public Offerings): This is the first time a corporation offers its shares to the public for purchase.

TFSA (Tax Free Savings Account): A type of investment account where you can contribute a certain amount every year, invest the amount, and pay zero tax on the growth of the account.

Other Investments

Currency Pair: A pair of two currencies that are traded against each other on the market.

Digital Wallet: A wallet where you store cryptocurrency.

Business Ownership

Business Plan: This is a comprehensive document that you put together that reviews all the different aspects of the business you want to start.

Shareholders: Everyone who owns a piece of a corporation.

Risk Tolerance

Risk: The possibility of losing the value of your investment.

ABOUT THE AUTHOR

Akinwale emigrated to Canada from Nigeria in 1999 to pursue a career as a stockbroker. While studying for the Canadian Securities Course, he discovered the financial planning profession. He began his career at Chartwell Securities and then worked with two prestigious investment firms and a bank, Aim/Trimark Investments, TD Investment Services, and TD Canada Trust, between 1999 and 2006 where he did everything from buying and selling investment products to loans and mortgages for individuals and businesses.

He became a financial planner at the Bank of Montreal in 2006, where he advised both mid- and high-net-worth clients in making investment decisions and planning for their retirement. By 2015, he had a portfolio of $52 million in assets under management.

Akinwale has a private financial planning practice, he teaches about finance in his community and manages the finances of a church and charity.

He is a public speaker, an avid investor and businessman, who within fifteen years of being in Canada, owned and co-owned several rental properties. He is director and shareholder in several businesses in Canada and the US.

His love for financial planning led him to teach a series of Money Management classes quarterly in the community and Financial Literacy classes in different parts of the Greater Toronto Area. He likes to explain complex financial concepts in simple everyday terms. As a Certified Financial Planner, He was an ambassador of FP Canada (the Financial Planning Standards Council), where he represented the council at several universities and colleges in Ontario to intending students of the financial planning profession between 2015 and 2017.

Akinwale has a BSc degree in Economics from the University of Lagos, an MSc in Finance from Walden University in Minnesota, and he is a Certified Financial Planner - CFP®

He is married with two beautiful daughters and has a home in Ajax, Ontario. Canada.

.